Food and Health
in Early Childhood

Food and Health
in Early Childhood

A Holistic Approach

Deborah Albon and Penny Mukherji

Los Angeles • London • New Delhi • Singapore

First published 2008

SAGE Publications Ltd
1 Oliver's Yard
55 City Road
London EC1Y 1SP

SAGE Publications Inc.
2455 Teller Road
Thousand Oaks, California 91320

SAGE Publications India Pvt Ltd
B 1/I 1 Mohan Cooperative Industrial Area
Mathura Road
New Delhi 110 044

SAGE Publications Asia-Pacific Pte Ltd
33 Pekin Street #02-01
Far East Square
Singapore 048763

Library of Congress Control Number: 2007936018

British Library Cataloguing in Publication data

A catalogue record for this book is available from the British Library

ISBN 978-1-4129-4721-3
ISBN 978-1-4129-4722-0 (pbk)

Typeset by C&M Digitals, Pvt Ltd, Chennai, India
Printed in Great Britain by T.J. International, Padstow, Cornwall
Printed on paper from sustainable resources

Contents

About the Authors   vii

Acknowledgements   viii

Preface   ix

1   Policy Development   1

Philanthropic concern (pre-1906)   2

A residual service (1906–Second World War)   3

A universal service (1944–79)   5

A return to the market (1980–96)   7

Safeguarding futures (1997 onwards)   10

2   Nutrition, Health and Development   18

An introduction to nutrients and food groups   19

The role of nutrition in the holistic development

of adults and children   25

Food sensitivity   28

Food additives   30

Obesity   31

3   Healthy Eating Guidelines   36

Healthy eating guidelines for adults   36

Healthy eating guidelines for conception and pregnancy   41

Providing food and drink for infants 0–1 year   46

Providing food and drink for children 1–5 years

(nursery guidelines)   54

Providing food and drink for children 5–8 years

(school guidelines)   57

4   Health Inequalities   61

Global poverty and health inequalities   61

Countries in transition and the effect of globalization   64

Health inequalities in Europe and the UK   67

Health inequalities and children's nutrition   70

Nutritional inequalities within families   73

5   Food, Eating and Emotion   77

The physiological processes underlying eating behaviour   77

Impulsivity and eating behaviour   80
Stress, depression and eating   81
The influence of early feeding experiences   83
Feading and eating disorders   87
Promoting positive attitudes towards food in early
years settings   90

6 **Food, Culture and Identity**   **95**
The symbolic significance of food and eating   95
Food, identity and religion   98
Food, identity and ethnicity   101
Food, identity and the 'green' or ethical
consumer perspective   104
Food, identity and class   105
Food, identity and gender   106
Children becoming part of the wider world   109

7 **Promoting Healthy Eating in Early**
   Childhood Settings   **115**
Why should we promote healthy eating in the early years?   116
What do we mean by health promotion?   116
Promoting healthy eating and the early years curriculum   120
Listening to children   127
Involving parents in promoting healthy eating   129
Developing a health promotion programme   131

8 **Multidisciplinary Working**   **135**
Why is multidisciplinary working important in the area
of children's food and eating?   136
What do we mean by multidisciplinary working?   140
Benefits and barriers to multidisciplinary working   143
Researching children's food and eating – the importance
of multidisciplinary working   147

Glossary   151
References   154
Index   165

About the Authors

Deborah Albon has worked as a nursery nurse, teacher and manager in a range of early childhood settings. Her research interests are primarily around food and drink provisioning and play in early childhood settings as well as in the home. Deborah has published a range of articles in this area and is currently engaged in research for a PhD. She works as Senior Lecturer in Early Childhood Studies at London Metropolitan University.

Penny Mukherji is an established author who has been involved in the education and training of early childhood professionals for over 20 years. After setting up a Foundation Degree in Early Childhood in a further education college, Penny is now lecturing on the Early Childhood Studies Degree at London Metropolitan University. Penny has a health background and her areas of interest include the health and well-being of young children and care and education of children under 3.

Acknowledgements

We would like to thank our families for their endless encouragement and support when writing this book.

We would also like to thank the Pre-School Learning Alliance, Alicha Doyle and Jan Turner for their initial help with the book and the Food Standards Agency for their assistance with Chapter 3.

Finally, we would like to thank the team at Sage for the enthusiasm and support they have given in the writing of this book.

Preface

Food and eating, for many people, is regarded as one of the great pleasures in life. It is something that is shared, albeit differently, across cultures and throughout human history. Understanding, preparing, cooking and sharing food for and with children from birth to 8 years is something that we as authors wish to celebrate in this book. However, we recognize that issues relating to food and eating are various and complex. After all, knowledge of nutrition and a healthy diet does not guarantee that people's food-related behaviour follows suit. Food and eating is a complex interplay of physiology, psychology, ethics and values, cultural expectation and symbolic meaning, to name but a few. Thus, it is an area that crosses many professional disciplines as well as theoretical approaches (Albon, 2005). As many of you will be aware, multidisciplinary approaches to working with children and families form much of public policy at the present time. This book is a timely look at an important area of practice through a variety of theoretical lenses.

Aims of this book

In order to explore a range of perspectives on food and health in early childhood, this book aims to:

▶ develop your knowledge and understanding about the crucial role food and drink play in young children's health and development. Children's earliest years are known to be the optimum time for developing healthy eating habits as well as for laying down the foundations for good health as an adult

▶ introduce you to a range of perspectives on food and eating, drawing on approaches from health studies, nutritional science, education, psychology, anthropology, social policy, sociology and cultural studies, for instance. In other words, this book is broader in scope than purely being a book looking at health and nutrition: our aim is to encourage you to think about food and eating through a range of theoretical lenses

▶ consider issues of equality and inclusion in relation to food and eating, such as how gender, race, ethnicity, class, religion and disability, impact upon our understanding and practice in this area

▸ encourage you to reflect on your professional practice with young children in relation to food and eating. In addition, you will be encouraged to reflect on your own attitudes towards food and eating

▸ encourage you to reflect on the increasing number of policy initiatives around food and health and the implication of these for early years practice, not least the need for multidisciplinary working.

A key aim for us is to convey our enthusiasm and commitment to developing quality provision for young children and their families in the area of food and eating – an area, we feel, that has tended to be neglected until recently. The concept of 'health' that underpins this book is a broad one. Generally, most health practitioners believe that health is not just the absence of disease, but includes the presence of the social, cultural, spiritual, mental and emotional aspects of life (Mukherji, 2005). We hope this broad conception of health is reflected in the range of material we have drawn upon in writing this book.

Organization of the book

The book is organized into eight chapters, each reflecting different perspectives on food and health in early childhood. Throughout the book you are encouraged to make links between your own beliefs and values, early years practice, and the theories introduced in the book in the form of reflection points, case studies and activities. Each chapter identifies key learning that will be introduced, further reading and useful web sites, and there is also a full glossary near the end of the book (glossary terms are emboldened in the text). We use the term 'early years practitioner' in the book to mean teachers and nursery nurses, that is, professionals who work with children under the age of 8 years in contexts such as nurseries, children's centres and schools.

We hope that this book will quite literally provide 'food for thought' in relation to young children and their family's diet and dietary behaviours, and encourage you to think about a range of perspectives on food and eating. We further hope that in reading this book, you will be inspired to reflect on your own attitudes towards food and eating as well as early years practice and share our passion and commitment to developing this fundamentally important area of early years practice.

Policy Development

> This chapter looks at the development of public policy in relation to children's food and eating. It charts the move from the view that what children eat is the private concern of the family, with philanthropic support for the most impoverished, to one of a universal service in the mid-1940s. The chapter also discusses the near reversal of such policy in the 1980s and the recent moves to seeing policy as part of broader strategies aimed at safeguarding children's futures, such as health promotion strategies and policies aimed at ecological sustainability.

Practice in relation to young children's food and eating does not occur in a vacuum. Public policy provides the framework within which practice is embedded and reflects cultural attitudes towards food and eating; something that is looked at in detail in Chapter 6 of this book. But public policy is not static. It changes according to historical and political circumstances, which emphasize different roles and responsibilities of the state, the family and children, and has changed as anxiety over children's diets has moved from alarm over lack of food to concerns about the excess and nutritional composition of the food in children's diets (Gustafsson, 2003). Much of the chapter charts the development of the school-meals service. However, provision of food and drink for children under 5 years in day care or nursery education has been less subject to state intervention, possibly highlighting the lack of a universal, state provided, full day-care and education service for children under 5 in the UK. Yet this is a crucial part of practice as an increasing number of young children receive their three main meals a day in such settings (Caroline Walker Trust, 2006).

This chapter aims to trace the development of policy in relation to young children's food and eating, highlighting the following key periods:

▸ Philanthropic concern (pre-1906)

▸ A residual service (1906–Second World War)

▸ A universal service (1944–79)

▸ A return to the market (1980–96)

▸ Safeguarding futures (1997 onwards)

Philanthropic concern (pre-1906)

The advent of compulsory schooling in 1870 highlighted the extent of malnutrition in the school population (Rose and Falconer, 1992). Passmore and Harris (2004) point out that school-meals provision began to be argued for on education as opposed to health grounds, because there were concerns that children would be unable to benefit from the state education system owing to malnutrition. The early childhood pioneer, Margaret McMillan, believed it was indefensible to expect a hungry child to learn, and focused upon the health inequalities that existed between the rich and the poor, saying, 'Below every strike, concealed behind legislation of every order, there is this fact – the higher nutrition of the favoured few compared with the balked childhood of the majority' (McMillan, quoted in Steedman, 1990: 15).

This echoes broader concerns, which ultimately lead to the development of school-meals provision. The 1899–1902 Boer War highlighted the number of recruits who were unfit to fight owing to malnutrition. This resulted in the setting up of a Royal Commission on Physical Deterioration, which was also a prime mover in the development of the 1906 Education (Provision of Meals) Act. Young (2002) also points out how the school meals service developed as a response to the dire social conditions experienced by the growing industrialized city populations. He discusses the experience in Scotland where, in the 1870s, there were Day Industrial Schools that were known as 'Feeding Schools', which provided at least one hot meal a day. If parents could not pay, the cost was met by charitable institutions. It should also be noted that in 1879 Manchester was one of the first cities in England to provide meals for poor and malnourished children.

The growth in the public provision of food for poor children is indicative of the way that philanthropic support was beginning to be challenged as the foremost means of alleviating poverty. Young (2002) notes that at the beginning of the twentieth century the burgeoning Labour movement and working-class, socialist agitation had led the then Liberal government to introduce policies such as National Insurance. The introduction of the school-meals service could arguably be seen as part of other welfare reforms of the period. Moreover, there was a feeling that school-meals provision could also have social advantages such as inculcating good manners and cleanliness, both deemed as deficient in the working-class child (Young, 2002).

Young (2002: 8–9) summarizes the key factors that led to the introduction of statutory school-meals provision as:

▸ An inducement to increase attendance at school

▸ A mechanism for increasing the stature and improving the health of the population

▸ A means of reducing crime and antisocial behaviour

- A means of inculcating good habits and manners
- A prerequisite for children to take full advantage of the education being provided
- A means of reducing the ill effects of privation on children during war-time
- A free service for those identified as most needy.

However, it is important to stress that despite the multitude of reasons that led to the development of the school-meals service, some people were strongly against it. The provision of meals was believed to usurp traditional family responsibility and the duty each family had to nurture their own children (Gustafsson, 2003).

A residual service (1906–Second World War)

Initially, the school-meals service developed as a service for the most impoverished children. The Education (Provision of Meals) Act of 1906 gave statutory authority to local education authorities (LEAs) to provide school meals. However we should be careful not to confuse this with a *duty* to provide meals for children. Until the Second World War, only 25,000 meals per year were provided even though there were 6 million children in school (Rose and Falconer, 1992).

Children who received a free dinner were often given a lesser quality dinner than those who paid and sometimes even ate separately (Passmore and Harris, 2004). The emphasis was on the quantity of food as opposed to the quality of the school dinner, as can be seen in this infant menu supplied by the Alexandra Trust for London County Council in 1906 (you can view it in full on http:// learningcurve. pro.gov.uk/britain1906-18/g2/cs2/g2cs2s3.htm) an extract of which is below.

Dinner menus for infants

- Stewed beef or mutton, suet roll, potatoes and bread
- Beef stewed with peas, suet roll, potatoes and bread
- Mutton stewed with haricot beans, steamed potatoes, bread and suet pudding
- Rice, tapioca, macaroni or barley pudding with two slices of sultana bread and butter
- Stew – very fine mince

▸ Baked custard, with bread and butter

▸ Savoury custard, with bread and butter

Breakfast menus

▸ Cocoa, porridge and two slices of bread and butter

▸ Cocoa, three slices of bread and dripping

▸ Hot milk and bread, two slices of bread and jam or marmalade

---

Reflection point

Look at the menu above. Does this menu reflect the kinds of food on offer to children at nursery or school today? In what ways does it differ?

Sharp (1992) notes that at the start of the First World War (1914), central government gave a 50 per cent grant for school meals, whereas previously money had come from local taxation within an expenditure limit set by central government. This resulted in a dramatic increase in the numbers of children receiving a meal, from 160,000 to 500,000. This grant was cut in the post-First World War period, which resulted in lower take-up of the provision, and in the 1930s there was increased targeting of school-meals provision to those deemed most needy, in order to direct scarce resources most efficiently. It was also during this time that the Milk Marketing Board introduced the School Milk Scheme, which ensured that poor and malnourished children received a third of a pint of free milk daily and those who were able to afford it were able to receive it at cost price (Passmore and Harris, 2004).

Activity

For those children who received a free school meal, this had a significant impact on their health. Look at the National Archive web site (see http://learningcurve.pro.gov.uk/britain1906-18/g2/cs2/g2cs24b.htm). You will see a graph that charts the increase and decrease in weight of a group of children in 1907. Take a few moments to look at how the weight of these children decreased during the school holidays. It serves as a stark reminder that malnourishment due to lack of food was a real concern for families living in poverty during this period.

Whilst this period of school-meals reform is characterized by its concern for the most impoverished children, the development of the school-meals service was also indicative of the increase in state interest and intervention in the private lives of the population (Gustafsson, 2003).

A universal service (1944–79)

The Second World War heralded a dramatic shift in policy. It is important to see this shift as part of the wider package of welfare reforms introduced in the 1940s such as the development of the National Health Service. Rose and Falconer (1992) highlight how the development of the welfare state in the post-war period emphasized the importance of collective, free provision of services as an expression of social solidarity.

Sharp (1992) argues that there were four key factors that impacted upon school-meals policy in this period:

1   Domestic rationing, brought in as a result of food shortages, did not take into account the particular needs and requirements of children. School meals were a way of ensuring children got a nourishing meal each day.

2   Wartime bombing led to large-scale movements of the population, such as the evacuation of children. This led to the development of large civic catering facilities.

3   Women were needed to work as part of the war effort, so school meals were seen as a key strategy in maximizing women's employment because women might be encouraged into employment in the comforting knowledge that their children were being fed while they were away.

4   A new policy of Family Allowance had been developed and this benefit included free school meals and milk as accompanying benefits.

In 1941 central government gave a 95 per cent grant to LEAs in order to fund the provision of school meals and there was a national campaign to expand the service (Passmore and Harris, 2004). Whilst it might be easy to skim over figures like this, it is important to think carefully about what they signify: central government grants for the funding of the service on this scale were unprecedented and are an expression of the importance that was placed on meals provision at that time. In the same year, the Board of Education Circular 1571 set the first nutritional standards for school meals. These specified the quantities of protein and fat the meal should provide, reflecting the influence of rationing (Passmore and Harris, 2004).

The 1944 (Butler) Education Act, section 49, altered the provision of school meals to children. Significantly, LEAs were now *obliged* to provide milk and a meal for all pupils who wanted one, in both primary and secondary schools and at a cost of no more than the ingredients unless entitled to free meals. It also legislated that post-war school buildings had to have a kitchen, which would enable meals to be cooked that were suitable for the children's main meal of the day (Passmore and Harris, 2004). Nutritional experts were keen that all children had access to nutrients and calories; indeed this was seen as an entitlement, although, in practice, these nutritional standards were not standardized for the whole of the UK until 1965 (Gustafsson, 2003).

The impact of this policy was a huge increase in the number of pupils receiving a school meal each day. When school-meals provision was at its height in the 1960s, two-thirds of children were receiving a school dinner (Rose and Falconer, 1992). Yet we should not be seduced into thinking that all children ate the dinner that was offered to them; even when collective provision was at its height, not all children ate it. Indeed the 1975 Department of Education and Science (DES) working party on nutrition in schools stated that children's diets in the home were now adequate in terms of daily intake of nutrients and there was recognition that there was wastage of school meals. The report urged LEAs to take into account the likes and dislikes of children when planning meals (Rose and Falconer, 1992).

Activity

Whilst some families have always paid for school meals, they do not pay the full cost of the dinner. We should remember that, in subsidizing school meals, wealthier families benefit as well as poorer families. Should the school-meals service aim to redistribute resources and concentrate on providing a service for those most in need, as seen in the 1906 provision? Alternatively, should the school-meals service promote social cohesion and provide a universal service i.e. for every child?

Spend some time listing arguments and counter-arguments for each position.

As well as developing a collectivist approach to school-meals provision, and we should note that the original intention was that it should develop into a free service for all irrespective of the ability to pay – albeit that this was never delivered – the 1940s saw the beginning of provision of milk for pregnant and breastfeeding mothers as well as young children. The Welfare Food Scheme was developed as a universal benefit and provided mothers and children under the age of 4 years with milk; 'national formula' for babies if not breastfed and milk for pregnant women and women who breastfed their children. In addition, all children in nurseries or day care were entitled to a third of a pint of milk daily (Buttriss, 2003). This universal service was another expression of the state having a strong role in providing welfare services for *all* its citizens, not just those who need them most.

In summing up this section, we can see that a strong state, providing universal services as a right of citizenship, characterizes this period. The Second World War had introduced government control of food, and indeed of other areas of social life, to an unprecedented level and the changes to school-meals provision in 1944 and the Welfare Food Scheme can both be positioned as an expression of social solidarity and an investment in the future citizenship of the nation.

A return to the market (1980–96)

Despite the optimism of the post-war period, there was a growing feeling that the collective provision of meals for young children was unnecessary, costly and, at its most extreme, damaging in terms of discouraging parents from taking responsibility for their own children. Rose and Falconer (1992: 350) quote Arthur Seldon, from the Institute of Economic Affairs, as proclaiming in the 1970s, 'Free or subsidized school meals do not teach parents to be less destitute, less irresponsible or less ignorant.'

From this, we can see a growth in thinking that for the vast majority of people, individual families should be responsible for the greater part of their children's care, unencumbered by the 'nanny state', which echoes concerns previously voiced when the 1906 Act was proposed. The welfare state, then, if we examine Seldon's quotation more deeply, was perceived to be part of the problem in creating welfare dependency, supposedly encouraging parents to abdicate their responsibilities for their own children. Thus, in stark contrast to the post-Second World War period, the state's role in relation to school meals was increasingly viewed as one of providing a safety net solely for the most needy.

The reining in of state provision in relation to children's dietary intake had begun prior to the 1980 Education Act. In 1971, Margaret Thatcher, when Secretary of State for Education, withdrew free school milk for children over the age of 7, unless there were medical grounds, which resulted in her being given the ignominious title of 'Thatcher the milk snatcher' (Rose and Falconer, 1992). However it was the 1980 Education Act, section 22, which signalled a significant change in policy direction in relation to school meals. Local education authorities had a duty to provide facilities where children could eat food brought from home, but only had a duty to provide a free meal for children whose parents qualified for means-tested benefits such as Social Security benefits. This was later withdrawn for some, when the 1986 Social Security Act, which took effect in 1988, withdrew the right to free school meals for those families receiving Family Credit; a benefit that had replaced Family Income

Supplement (Rose and Falconer, 1992). Gradually, the definition of those entitled to a free meal became narrower.

Crucially, the 1980 Education Act abolished the nutritional requirements of the school meal and its fixed price. Taste was seen as an individual decision for parents and children to make as opposed to a collective one made on behalf of parents and children by the state (Rose and Falconer, 1992), and the money savings this gained were proclaimed as a positive way of saving public money. Central government was no longer responsible for the price rises of school meals – this responsibility now fell to LEAs.

In 1988, another key policy change was the introduction of compulsory competitive tendering (CCT) as part of the Local Government Act 1986. Whilst on the surface this may not seem to relate to school meals, it was significant in introducing competitive tendering for catering contracts for the school-meals service. Thus, LEAs had to put services such as school meals out to tender and invite bids from a range of caterers, resulting in the growth of managerialism and governance, which developed in order to monitor the quality of services not directly provided by the state (Gustafsson, 2003).

It is important to see this shift in policy from a universal, state-provided service to one that is contracted out to private catering firms, in terms of broader concerns about the welfare state at this time. The Conservative government at this time, which reflected New Right or neo-liberal thinking, attacked welfare state provision for:

▸ *being inefficient and wasteful of resources* – as there was no incentive to keep costs down if monies came from central government as opposed to locally managed resources

▸ *lacking competition* – in the private sector, standards were perceived to be higher as people could choose from a range of options. Thus, poor suppliers of goods and services are driven out or improve the quality of their services in order to compete with more successful firms

▸ *being overly centralized* – the notion of the 'nanny state' and distrust in state institutions was contrasted with individual responsibility – for oneself and one's family. Thus, the state's role in relation to welfare provision was seen as that of providing a safety net for those most in need rather than a universal service

▸ *lacking choice* – collective, standardized, universal provision was contrasted with the possibility of diverse provision that could be more responsive to the needs of the consumer. Note the use of the word 'consumer' here, as government thinking celebrated the notion of there being a welfare consumer, *choosing* from a range of welfare options as opposed to being *allocated* a standardized service.

The principle of choice was deemed to be an important one and one that we can see evidence of in cafeteria-style dining rooms. However the Black Report (Townsend and Davidson, 1982) highlighted that free choice for young children around the food they wanted to eat was wrong as they might make unhealthy choices. Whilst this may not be too significant if the child receives a nutritious diet away from school, it may have a considerable negative impact on children living in poverty. Gustafsson (2003: 135) notes that the implementation of the 1980 Education Act, 'signals a shift in the vision of the child, from being a collective recipient of stipulated, standardized provision to an individual consumer capable of selecting from a range of alternatives.'

Reflection point

Reflect on the extent to which you think young children should be able freely to choose what they have to eat. Is the principle of free choice more important than that of equality of access to a healthy diet? Is there a middle ground whereby children have a range of healthy options to choose from? How might this work in practice? Are there disadvantages to this?

Passmore and Harris (2004) point out that alongside the changes in the way school meals were provided, by 1992 the Department of Health had developed a paper entitled 'The Health of the Nation', which set national targets for improving public health. Targets were set for diet and nutrition, such as lowering obesity and reducing coronary heart disease, and the role of schools in relation to children's food and eating was seen as needing to become one of health promotion. This linked to the World Health Organization's (WHO) first international conference on health promotion, which resulted in the Ottawa Charter (WHO, 1986). This marked a shift in thinking towards schools needing to become engaged with developing children's and young people's understanding, skills and attitudes about health and lifestyle in order to be able to make informed decisions.

Also significant during this period, was the ratification of the United Nations Convention on the Rights of the Child (UNCRC). Article 24 states that children have the right to health care, clean water to drink, nutritious food and a clean environment; thus enshrining a healthy diet as the right of *all* children. The UNCRC is important as it forms the basis for approaches to working with children, which include children as participants rather than passive recipients of services. In Chapter 7, we look at listening to children and health promotion more fully. However in this chapter, it should be noted that children's voices regarding their food and eating experiences at school or nursery are often absent in policy development (Gustafsson, 2003).

In summing up this period, we should not underestimate the shift in policy at this time. Passmore and Harris (2004) summarise the main points as follows:

▸ The provision of school meals became a discretionary local service, unless the child was entitled to a free meal

▸ The fixed price for school meals was removed

▸ Nutritional standards were abolished

▸ The entitlement of all to free milk was abolished

▸ School-meals services were subject to CCT.

Safeguarding futures (1997 onwards)

In April 2005, following a high-profile television series and the 'Feed me Better' campaign, Jamie Oliver's visit to Downing Street put school meals high on the government agenda. The contracting-out of catering services had resulted in a consumer-led service, where profitability was elevated over nutrition (Passmore and Harris, 2004) and Jamie Oliver's campaign highlighted the poor quality of much of the food on offer to children in schools.

However, it would be a mistake to believe that Jamie Oliver was the sole voice in advocating change. Nutritionists had been active for many years in lobbying the government to change its policy in relation to school meals (Buttriss, 2005) and the deregulation of the school-meals service as well as the reduction in the numbers of children entitled to free meals had led to the formation of a pressure group called the School Meals Campaign in 1992, comprising a range of other groups including Child Poverty Action Group (Gustafsson, 2003). In addition, an expert panel in Scotland produced the report *Hungry for Success* (Scottish Executive, 2002), which envisioned a better school-meals service. Whilst these groups were influential, perhaps they did not have Jamie Oliver's high media profile in galvanizing a degree of public support, not least from the national media. However, we should remember that his campaign barely touched on meal-time provision for children under 5 years.

In thinking about policy since the Labour election victory of 1997, it would be wrong to believe that there has been a significant shift away from the market principles expounded by the successive Conservative governments of the 1980s and 1990s. The language of the market, such as 'commissioning' services, still underpins much public policy, including that of policy in relation to young children and food. Noorani (2005) points out how since 1997 'Best Value' had replaced CCT in local authorities, who need to ensure that the quality and cost of services reflect what people want and can afford.

Further to this, the UK government has tended to be reluctant to legislate in the area of television advertising around unhealthy foods and drinks aimed at young children, particularly during children's prime viewing times: this has been viewed as a matter for parents to decide and a matter for voluntary discretion on the part of advertisers. This reluctance in turn could be viewed as unwillingness on the part of the government to interfere with private sector institutions. Scandinavian countries, for instance, have instituted a ban in this area (Gustafsson, 2003).

This attitude seems to be changing. On 31 March, 2007, restrictions on food advertising came into force in the UK, aimed at reducing the exposure of children to advertising of unhealthy foods. Companies wishing to advertise their food products during children's prime-time television are required to assess the nutritional composition of their product against the Food Standard Agency's Nutrient Profiling Model (www.food.gov.uk/news).

A return to nutritional standards

In 2001, the Department for Education and Employment (DFEE) reinstated minimum standards for school meals. This was as a result of the strong connection made between diet and disease, and the acknowledgement of the importance of a nutritious diet in safeguarding a healthy future for all children (Passmore and Harris, 2004). The 2001 standards focus on food and food groups as opposed to nutrients, unlike the Scottish initiative 'Hungry for Success', and set standards for pre-schools, primary schools and secondary schools (Buttriss, 2005). Chapter 3 looks in detail at new guidance around food in nurseries and schools.

Reflection point

It has been reported that in some schools where the menu for school lunches was changed to bring them in line with healthy eating guidelines, parents protested that their children were no longer eating the food provided and were going hungry. In one school, parents handed burgers, chips and fizzy drinks to their children though the school fence (Weaver, 2006). What can be done to prevent this sort of conflict?

In relation to childcare, National Standards for Childcare were published in 2000 in Wales, 2001 in England, and 2002 in Scotland. These standards apply to a range of early years provision:

▸ Full-day care

▸ Sessional care

 ▸ Crèches

 ▸ Out-of-school care

 ▸ Childminders.

Standard 8 looks at food and drink arrangements in childcare settings and offers guidance to providers as well as to inspectors. Providers need to ensure they have clear records of individual children's dietary needs; ensure there is access to fresh water and regular drinks and should provide healthy and nutritious meals and snacks for children, for instance. However, these standards are welcome, there is an assumption that all providers have an understanding of what 'healthy and nutritious' means, something that is not always borne out in practice (Caroline Walker Trust, 2006).

The Department of Health (2004c) document, *Choosing Health,* was committed to reviewing school lunch nutritional standards. Following this, the government has implemented a range of measures such as developing a School Food Trust as an advisory body and has charged the Office for Standards in Education (OFSTED) with looking at the meals on offer in schools as part of its inspection duties. Importantly, there has been a £235 million commitment from government to transform meals.

In addition to school-based initiatives, the Welfare Food Scheme introduced in 1940 was reviewed by the Committee on Medical Aspects of Food and Nutrition Policy (COMA) and in 2002 the Department of Health proposed a scheme called 'Healthy Start' to improve the nutritional health of women and young children. This programme is seen as complementing Sure Start programmes, which, amongst other aims, endeavour to ensure children have a healthy start in life through breastfeeding (www.surestart.gov.uk). 'Healthy Start' includes more than just milk, also cereal-based foods suitable for weaning as well as fruit. However, as Buttriss (2003) observes, parents may choose to obtain foods other than milk, and given the benefits of milk in preventing dental caries, need careful monitoring. In addition, Buttriss highlights how the Department of Health has developed a programme of public education to help support pregnant mothers and carers to make informed choices with the vouchers they receive. The vouchers cover the following categories:

 ▸ pregnant women

 ▸ children aged 0–6 months

 ▸ 6–12 months

 ▸ 1–5 years.

Policy at the present time also needs to be viewed more widely, as part of the Every Child Matters agenda (DfES, 2003), which identifies five key outcomes that are paramount to children's health and well-being:

1   Being healthy

2   Staying safe

3   Enjoying and achieving

4   Making a positive contribution

5   Economic well-being.

Healthy eating plays a key role in children's general health in both the short and long terms, and is a significant factor in the first of the outcomes. In addition to the Children Act 2004, the Ten Year Strategy for Childcare was announced in 2004, and aims to develop a high-quality national provision of childcare. The Caroline Walker Trust (2006: 16) argues that they would like 'the right of every child to good food to be a significant part of this new vision'. This is something we want to endorse.

In analysing policy direction at the current time, two further strands can be identified; health promotion and an ecological approach.

Health promotion

There has been a shift since the end of the 1980s towards seeing nurseries and schools as playing an important role in health promotion and this has continued to gather pace in the early twenty-first century. In 1997, a White Paper was published called *Excellence in Schools* (DfEE, 1998), which aimed to enable all schools to become 'healthy schools'. Further to this, in 1999, the Department of Health report, *Saving Lives: Our Healthier Nation* also highlighted the key role schools ought to play in educating children about health, including healthy eating, leading to the National Healthy School Standard (NHSS). By May 2001, 30 per cent of English schools had achieved NHSS, which involves meeting quality standards around specific topics, including educating children about healthier eating and food safety as part of the curriculum.

£45 million of Lottery Fund money has been allocated for healthy eating projects involving children, parents and local communities. Important projects highlighted by Buttriss (2005) include:

▸   Further development of the NHSS in order to emphasize whole-school approaches to diet and exercise

▸   The Food in Schools Programme, led by the Department of Health, but as a joint initiative with the DfES, of has developed a tool kit that was launched in April 2005. The tool kit aims to help schools towards the Healthy School standards and support the healthy living blueprint

▸   The five-a-day school fruit and vegetables scheme.

Activity

Carry out an online search at www.foodinschools.org.uk and look for information about projects around healthier lunch-boxes, growing clubs, healthier breakfast clubs, healthier cookery clubs, and many more.

In 2000, Passmore and Harris (2004) point out that the National Curriculum was altered in order to promote a wider role for Personal, Social and Health Education (PSHE). The aim was to teach children how to develop a healthier, safer lifestyle and to teach them about healthy eating. The *Early Years Foundation Stage* 2007 curriculum guidance (www.standards.dfes/gov.uk/eyfs) includes guidance around promoting positive attitudes and self-care in relation to healthy eating.

Given the amount of activity there has been around health promotion in recent years, we might conclude that the state is moving towards a model whereby children are educated about how they can safeguard their *own* futures by learning how to make healthy choices, such as around diet and exercise. This can be contrasted with the state making those healthy choices on their behalf – particularly once reaching adulthood, as seen in wartime rationing and the school-meals provision developed in the 1940s. This is also reflected in the education programme to support mothers in making informed choices with their 'Healthy Start' vouchers rather than merely assigning them food and drink. The distinction is an important one. It highlights the reluctance of the government, and indeed much of the population, to sacrifice the choice associated with being a consumer with that of being a recipient of allocated state provision. We need only to look at the outrage amongst some parents over the changes in school meals to reflect healthier eating options, to see evidence of this. Therefore, the role of government seems to have shifted to one of educating the public about healthy eating as opposed to making those healthy choices for them. In order to facilitate this, the government role has moved to one of *creating the right conditions* for these choices to be made, or an enabling role (see, for instance, DoH, 2004c). One aspect of this can be seen in the increasing importance placed on multidisciplinary working; something we look at in Chapter 8.

Ecological approaches

As well as the return to nutritional standards, the focus on health promotion and reforms to the Welfare Food Scheme, Morgan (2007) points to the development of an ecological approach to school food reforms. In 2005, the report 'Turning the Tables' was published, which recommended that food be procured in accordance with sustainable development principles, such as using local producers where possible (School Meals Review Panel, 2005). Morgan goes on to show how food plays a crucial role in the UK's sustainable development strategy. This ecological agenda can also be seen in the development of eco-schools (www. eco-schools.org.uk). This could be interpreted as another expression of the state's interest in safeguarding children's futures.

The final section in this chapter demonstrates that there has been a huge array of policy developments in relation to children and food in the past few years. There have been so many developments in such a short space of time and involving a range of different agencies that it is easy to feel exhausted when trying to keep abreast of them. Morgan (2007: 1) argues that the issue of school food is 'becoming a litmus test of the Labour government's avowed commitment to public health, social justice and sustainable development'. Whilst there have been positive moves forward since 1997, such as the reinstatement of nutritional standards for school meals, Gustafsson (2003) notes the absence of the child's voice in relation to public policy-making around school meals, despite the fact that they are the direct recipients of the service. As Chapters 5 and 6 demonstrate, food has a strong link to one's emotions and sense of identity, therefore transforming children's tastes and, consequently, diets will not happen overnight.

Summary

- ▸ The development of policy in the area of children and food has undergone shifts in focus, which reflect wider political and cultural attitudes towards the roles and responsibilities of the state, the family and the child

- ▸ Initially the 1906 Education (Provision of Meals) Act was introduced to ensure that the most impoverished children received a meal every school day enabling them to benefit from the relatively new national education system

- ▸ The post-Second World War period heralded universal, state provision of school meals and the Welfare Food Scheme for young children and pregnant and breastfeeding mothers. The numbers of children partaking of school meals increased dramatically and nutritional standards were stipulated by the state

- ▸ In 1980, the Education Act reversed the notion of a universal, state-provided service to one of a duty for local education authorities to provide a safety net service for those children receiving benefits entitling them to free meals. Nutritional standards were abolished. Later in the decade, school-meals services became subject to CCT

- ▸ Since 1997 there has been a plethora of policy in relation to children and food. Nutritional standards for school meals are now in place and there is an increasing focus on sustainability – an ecological approach to food and eating – and health promotion.

The chapter can be further summarized by way of a policy time line (Figure 1.1).

1906 The Education (Provision of Meals) Act introduced, giving authority to local education authorities (LEAs) to provide meals

1934 Free school milk introduced nationally

1941 Welfare Food Scheme introduced for children under 4 years and pregnant and breastfeeding mothers. Nutritional standards for school meals set nationally

1944 The 1944 Education Act, section 49, made it a duty for LEAs to provide school meals for all children who wanted one. Free school milk made available to all

1971 Entitlement to free school milk for children over 7 abolished

1980 Education Act, sections 22 and 23, gave LEAs the power to abolish school meals apart from for those children entitled to a free meal. Nutritional standards abolished

1986 Social Security Act means children whose families receive Family Credit are not entitled to a free school meal or milk

1988 LEAs had to put catering services out to compulsory competitive tendering (CCT) following 1986 Local Government Act

1992 Department of Health publishes 'The health of the nation' which includes public health targets around food and eating.

1998 *Excellence in Schools* published by the DfEE, aimed at helping schools become 'healthy schools'

1999 Department of Health report, *Saving Lives: Our Healthier Nation*, highlights the key role schools ought to play in educating children about health, including healthy eating, leading to the National Healthy School Standard (NHSS)

2000 Broadening of National Curriculum to include Personal, Social and Health Education

2001 National nutritional standards for school meals introduced. National Childcare standards, section 8, give guidance around the provision of food and drink in childcare settings

2002 Scottish Executive publishes *Hungry for Success*. Healthy Start replaces Welfare for Food Scheme and includes foods other than milk

2003 Birth to Three Matters includes 'A Healthy Child' as one of its four areas

2004 Department of Health publishes *Choosing Health*. Children Act 2004 implements the Every Child Matters' five outcomes, including 'Being Healthy'

2005 School Food Trust set up, comprising food experts, to advise the government. Food in schools tool kit introduced, which is intended to help schools towards the Healthy School standards and support the healthy living blueprint. The five-a-day school fruit and vegetables scheme is introduced. The government report 'Turning the tables' is published and recommends that food be procured in accordance with sustainable development principles

2006 New food-based standards, set by School Food Trust, introduced across all schools

2007 The Early Years Foundation Stage is finalized with explicit references to young children's food and eating

Figure 1.1 A time line of policy developments in relation to children, food and eating

Discussion points

▸ Should young children contribute to the development of food and meal-time policy? How can their views be accessed?

▸ To what extent should the state impose nutritional requirements on packed lunches brought from home?

▸ If you think the state ought to impose nutritional requirements on packed lunches brought from home, should this be monitored and enforced? If so, how?

Further reading

Gustafsson, U. (2003) 'School meals policy: the problem with governing children', in E. Dowler and C. Jones-Finer (eds), *The Welfare of Food: Rights and Responsibilities in a Changing World*. Oxford: Blackwell.

Passmore, S. and Harris, G. (2004) 'Education, health and school meals: a review of policy changes in England and Wales over the last century', *Nutrition Bulletin*, 29(3): 221–7.

Useful web sites

(If you have any trouble following the links given in this book, please go back to the web site's homepage and search for the topic in question from there.)

www.foodinschools.org.uk (accessed 25 July 2007).

www.nationalarchives.gov.uk (search the web site for historical material relating to food and eating) (accessed 25 July 2007).

Nutrition, Health and Development

In this chapter the fundamental role that nutrition plays in the health, growth and development of young children is explored. The chapter will investigate evidence that suggests that early nutritional experiences have long-term consequences for individuals throughout their lives. The links between a child's nutritional status and learning is emphasized. In order to understand the concepts investigated within this chapter, a brief introduction to nutrition is included, together with a discussion as to how growth and development can be monitored and assessed. The particular challenges of childhood obesity and food allergies will be investigated.

All of us involved in the professional care of children and young people have a responsibility to promote their health and well-being, as was emphasized in the government Green Paper *Every Child Matters* where one of the outcomes for children is: 'Being healthy, enjoying good physical and mental health and living a healthy lifestyle' (DfES, 2003: 6). This outcome was later enshrined in the 2004 Children Act.

This chapter takes a bio-medical look at food and introduces you to some of the key topics in the subject of dietetics, the study of the health-related aspects of nutrition. This is an **empirical** approach to the subject; other chapters will be looking at food and eating from a variety of different perspectives. Nutrition plays a vital role in children's health, growth and development. A sound knowledge of nutrition and the principles that underpin planning for children's nutritional needs is essential for early years practitioners because for many children in our care the nutrition they receive from us comprises the majority of their food intake. Good nutrition in the early years not only promotes healthy growth and development, but also prevents ill health in adulthood and contributes to effective learning and academic achievement.

The following key areas are explored in this chapter:

▸ An introduction to nutrients and food groups

▸ The role of nutrition in the holistic development of adults and children

▸ Food sensitivity

▸ Food additives

▸ Obesity.

An introduction to nutrients and food groups

Hardly a day goes by without an aspect of nutrition being given coverage in the media, be it on the television news or in the newspaper. Words such as 'calorie', 'saturated fat', 'protein' and 'vitamin' are all part of our everyday vocabulary. Although healthy eating is a common topic of conversation today, the science of nutrition is relatively new. From the Middle Ages, there was a recognition that one's diet played a role in one's health, but it was not until the seventeenth to eighteenth centuries that there began to be an understanding of the role of individual **nutrients** within the body. For example, it was Lind in 1747 who is credited with running one of the first ever clinical trials when he demonstrated that citrus fruits could mitigate against the effects of scurvy (Hackett, 2006). It was in the late nineteenth/early twentieth centuries that the concept of essential nutrients was developed and the identification of vitamins and minerals important for health was established.

In attempting to outline the essential components that are needed to keep us healthy, two main approaches have been used. One approach, the nutrient approach, aims to identify and quantify the nutrients we need for healthy growth and development and to suggest foods that contain these nutrients. The other approach places less emphasis on individual nutrients, but looks at the different types of foods we need to include in our diet to ensure a ready supply of important nutrients. This is the **food group** approach.

Activity

In a book such as this it is only possible to give the barest of outlines to these two approaches; fortunately there are very good resources to be found on the Internet.

The British Nutrition Foundation www.nutrition.org.uk/ has a good section on the important nutrients in our diet.

The BBC www.bbc.co.uk/health/healthy_living/nutrition has a good section on food groups.

The nutrient approach

The main nutrients needed for healthy growth and development are divided into two main groups. The **macronutrients** (fats, proteins and carbohydrates) are substances needed in significant quantities in our diets and supply energy. **Micronutrients** (vitamins and minerals) are substances that are only needed in minuscule quantities in our diet to keep us healthy. In addition water and fibre are also essential.

The British Nutrition Foundation (2004) gives the following information about nutrients.

Carbohydrate

Carbohydrate is a macronutrient, providing energy in our diet. There are two main types of carbohydrates: sugars and complex carbohydrates. Sugars that occur naturally, within the cells of foods, are known as intrinsic sugars. Foods containing intrinsic sugars include whole fruits and some vegetables. Extrinsic sugars are those that are not incorporated into the cell structure of foods. These include lactose or milk sugar and sugar found in fruit juice, honey and refined sugar used in cooking and in confectionery.

Complex carbohydrates are of two main types. The first is starch which is found in starchy vegetables, such as potatoes, and foods derived from cereals, such as bread and pasta. The second type of complex carbohydrate is fibre. Fibre is derived from plants (fruits, vegetables, nuts, grains, and so on) and is primarily formed from cellulose cell walls. Fibre is not digested in the small intestine of the body.

The carbohydrate that we consume is ultimately broken down into glucose which is used as energy/fuel by the body's tissues. One gram of carbohydrate will produce approximately 4 kcal of energy. Energy comes from a variety of foods that contain the macronutrients carbohydrate, fat and protein. Alcohol also supplies energy. Energy is stored in the body as fat, so if too much carbohydrate is consumed, it will be converted into fat and we will gain weight. Too little carbohydrate in the diet will mean that the body will use the fat and protein in the diet as fuel, together with the fat reserves.

Protein

Protein is needed for growth and repair in the body and also supplies energy (1 gram of protein will supply 4 kcal of energy). Protein is found in foods derived from animals, such as meat, milk, fish and eggs. It can also be found in foods from plants, such as cereals, pulses, nuts and seeds.

All our body tissues, organs and muscles contain protein which is made from building blocks called amino acids. When we eat foods containing protein, the amino acids are released and are used, in different combinations, to build the proteins that the body needs. The body can make some amino acids for itself, without having to have obtained them from the diet; however, there are a small number of amino acids that the body cannot synthesize. These amino acids are known as indispensable or essential amino acids. The British Nutrition Foundation (BNF) identifies the following as essential: leucine, isoleucine, valine, threonine, methionine, phenylalanine, tryptophan and lysine. For children, histidine is also considered to be an essential amino acid (BNF, 2004).

Foods that contain protein from animal sources are more likely to contain all the essential amino acids that the body needs than foods from plant sources. However, it is perfectly possible for vegetarians to eat only non-animal sources of protein and remain healthy. This is because by eating protein from two different plant sources at the same time, all the essential amino acids may be supplied. For example, eating a cereal such as rice, together with a pulse such as lentils will provide all the essential amino acids.

Fats

Although we only need a little fat in our diet, it is an important nutrient. It is a concentrated source of energy, 1 gram of fat giving approximately 9 kal. Fat is, therefore, a valuable source of energy for babies and infants who have small stomachs and need proportionally more energy-rich foods than older children and adults. Brain tissue comprises 60 per cent fat (Brooks et al., 2000), where the essential fatty acids linoleic acid and alpha linolenic acid are involved in nerve formation. Fat is also essential as a carrier for the fat soluble vitamins A, D, E and K.

There are several different types of fat:

▸ *Saturated fatty acids*, found in milk, meat, dairy products and eggs. Saturated fats are solid at room temperature and are known to raise the level of cholesterol in the blood.

▸ *Monounsaturated fatty acids*, fluid at room temperature, are found in meat, cereals, avocados, olive oil, sunflower oil and nuts. They are considered to be beneficial to health.

▸ *Polyunsaturated fatty acids*, also oils at room temperature, include omega 3 and omega 6. They are known to have a positive effect on cardiovascular health. Foods containing polyunsaturated fatty acids include grain products, fish and sea food (herring, salmon, mackerel and halibut), soybeans, fish oil and soft margarines.

▸ *Trans fatty acids*, are rarely found naturally in the food we eat. These fats are manufactured by adding hydrogen to oils, often in an effort to increase shelf life or raise the temperature at which the fat can be used for cooking. There is mounting evidence that trans fats are harmful and there are moves for manufacturers to disclose the presence of trans fats in their products.

The body can make all the fatty acids it needs except two, known as the essential fatty acids, linoleic acid and alpha linolenic acid. These two nutrients must be supplied by the diet and the best sources are oily fish and fish oil supplements. The meat or eggs of animals fed a diet high in fish oils will also contain significant amounts of the essential fatty acids.

The consumption of too much fat will lead to it being laid down as **adipose tissue**, ultimately leading to overweight and obesity.

Vitamins

These are micronutrients that are only needed in minute quantities in our diet to promote health and without which we will begin to show signs of illness. The knowledge of these complex substances is developing all the time and the number of vitamins identified is steadily increasing. Traditionally the vitamins have been divided into two: the fat soluble vitamins and the water soluble vitamins.

▸ Fat soluble vitamins include vitamins A, D, E and K.

▸ Water soluble vitamins include vitamins C, B1, B2, B6, B12, niacin and folate.

Activity

Look up the vitamins mentioned above. Devise a chart that gives information about the role of each vitamin in the body, the best food sources and the possible consequences of not getting enough of the particular vitamin in the diet.

If one eats a healthy well-balanced diet one should be able to get all the vitamins needed to maintain health without resorting to supplements. The exceptions to this are pregnant women, who are advised to take folate supplements, and infants, who are recommended to be given vitamin drops.

Minerals

Minerals are chemical elements required by the body in small amounts for a variety of functions. Minerals form the structural basis of the bones, are essential components of body fluids and are vital for the normal functioning of enzymes and nerves. The minerals required by the body can be divided into two groups: minerals needed in measurable amounts, and trace elements, needed only in minute quantities.

▸ Minerals needed in measurable amounts include calcium, magnesium, phosphorous, sodium, potassium and iron. Of these, only iron is likely to be deficient in children in the UK.

▸ Trace elements include zinc, iodine, fluoride, selenium, copper, chromium, manganese, molybdenum and boron. Of these, only fluoride is likely to be deficient in children in the UK.

Activity

Look up calcium, iron and fluoride on the Internet. Devise a chart that gives information about the role of each mineral in the body, the best food sources and the possible consequences of not getting enough of the particular mineral in the diet.

Dietary fibre

Dietary fibre, sometimes known as non-starch polysaccarides, is a complex substance, mainly consisting of plant cell walls. It can, therefore, be found in fruit, vegetables, pulses, grains, nuts, and so on. Fibre cannot be digested by the small intestine but it can be digested by micro organisms that live in the large intestine. Although much of the fibre we consume passes through the body undigested, it has a valuable role to play in our health.

▸ Fibre helps prevent constipation.

▸ Fibre helps lower blood cholesterol and glucose level.

A diet low in fibre has been implicated in the onset of bowel cancer and diverticulitis. Small children, however, should not be given too much fibre in their diet as their stomachs are small and they need concentrated forms of energy. Foods containing too much fibre fill them up without supplying the nutrients they need. Guidelines for children are discussed in the next chapter.

Water

Our bodies are made of between 60 and 70 per cent water, and regular fluid intake is vital for health. The various functions of water include:

▸ lubricating eyes and joints

▸ helping us swallow

▸ acting as a medium for biological processes and chemical reactions

▸ helping get rid of waste products

▸ forming the basis of body fluids such as blood and **lymph**

▸ helping regulate body temperature.

The amount of water we need varies according to the weather, the amount of physical activity we undertake, what we are eating and our age. Most of us probably do not drink enough water (or drinks containing water); feelings of thirst arise only after we have become dehydrated.

The food group approach

Although nutritionists are able to tell us exactly how much of each nutrient we need in our diets, this approach is not easy to apply in everyday life. When advising us on healthy eating the experts divide foods into groups that supply similar nutrients.

In the UK the government organization, the Food Standards Agency 2007 (www. food.gov.uk) recommends a set of dietary guidelines called 'The Eatwell Plate'. The guidelines divide foods into five main groups:

▸ bread, Rice, pasta and others starchy foods

▸ fruit and vegetables

▸ milk and dairy foods

▸ meat, fish, eggs, beans and other non-dairy sources of protein

▸ foods and drinks high in fat and/or sugar.

These guidelines are explained further in Chapter 3.

Activity

Using the information about nutrients in the preceding section, identify the main nutrients in each of the food groups outlined above. Then check your understanding by looking at the information on the Food Standards Agency web site. www.food.gov.uk/multimedia/pdfs/bghbooklet.pdf

The role of nutrition in the holistic development of adults and children

'Out of 100 children born today 30 will suffer from malnutrition' (UNICEF, 2006). At the time of writing there are crises in East Africa, especially Kenya, where over 8 million people are on the brink of starvation owing to severe drought, crop failure and loss of livestock. Of those affected, 1.6 million are children under the age of 5. In West Africa the United Nations Children's Fund is appealing for £16 million to reach children affected by the nutrition crisis in Burkina Faso, Mali, Mauritania and Niger. The nutrition crisis primarily affects children under the age of 2, who suffer from low birth weight, poor breastfeeding practices and inadequate access to basic services. In addition, a recent health survey showed that 48 per cent of children in Malawi show signs of malnutrition; 5 per cent of these are severely malnourished. In Darfur, Sudan, lack of food and water affects 1.4 million children under the age of 18 (from the UNICEF web site, www.unicef.org.uk).

In the **majority world**, many families struggle to find the resources to feed children adequately, and the most prevalent form of **malnutrition** is due to insufficient food being available. In the UK some children are also malnourished, but the cause is more likely to be the excessive consumption of food (for the child's energy requirements) or an unbalanced diet, lacking in essential nutrients.

Increasingly in the UK, we are becoming concerned about the adverse health effects of poor diet. In a study by Rayner and Scarborough (2005: 1054) it was estimated that 'food related ill health is responsible for about 10 percent of **morbidity** and **mortality** in the UK and costs the NHS about £6 billion annually'. They conclude that:

> The burden of food related ill health measured in terms of mortality and morbidity is similar to that attributable to smoking. The cost to the NHS is twice the amount attributable to car, train, and other accidents, and more than twice that attributable to smoking. The vast majority of the burden is attributable to unhealthy diets rather than to food borne diseases. (Ibid.)

The effect on health of lack of food has, of course, been understood from prehistoric times, but it took the development of nutrition as a science before a fuller understanding of the role that food plays in maintaining health was achieved. As was noted in the previous section, it was not until the early 1900s that vitamins were discovered. The consequences of poor nutrition were brought home to the UK government in 1917 when it was discovered that

41 per cent of men called up for military service were unfit, with poor nutrition being a huge factor (Chamberlain, 2004). The science of nutrition was further promoted at the time of the Second World War when food was rationed and the government needed advice on how best to keep the population healthy on limited food supplies (see Chapter 1).

Since the end of the Second World War there have been significant changes in the food we eat. From eating fresh food in season that had to be prepared at home, we now have a wide variety of foods available all year from around the world. There is a greater consumption of prepared food and an increase in the amount of fat and sugar in our diet. Affluence has given us the opportunity to indulge in 'fast food', and sugar-rich 'fizzy' drinks are now a regular part of our diet. This, together with a lack of exercise, has led to a rise in the number of adults and children who are overweight and obese.

Reflection point 〰

How have your diet and lifestyle changed since you were a child? Those of you who are relatively young may not think that your diet has changed that much, but some of you may have seen great changes. If you can, ask someone who lived through the Second World War in the UK and experienced rationing. What are their memories? Some of you may have spent your early years in another country. In what ways have your diet changed?

There is much research evidence about the effect that a poor diet has on health. As well as the health risks associated with obesity, discussed later on in this chapter, there are other common health conditions that are related to poor diet. These include:

▸ *Oral diseases*. Under-nutrition is associated with an increase in gum disease and developmental defects of the enamel. Excess sugar in the diet is implicated in the formation of **dental caries** and the acid in soft drinks is implicated in the erosion of tooth enamel (Moynihan, 2005).

▸ *Iron deficiency anaemia*. This is a disease caused by a deficiency of iron in the diet, which is needed to form red blood cells. Iron is found in red meat, pulses and leafy green vegetables. Iron deficiency anaemia can make people feel tired, irritable and less able to concentrate. In children, it can affect behaviour, development and school achievement. Iron deficiency anaemia is probably the most common nutritional deficiency in the world – in the UK 3 per cent of boys and 8 per cent of girls aged 4–6 years, 1 per cent of boys and 4 per cent of girls aged 7–10 years, and

1 per cent of boys and 9 per cent of girls aged 15–18 years are anaemic (Ruston et al., 2004).

▸ *Vitamin D deficiency.* Vitamin D is a fat-soluble vitamin found primarily in dairy products and oily fish such as salmon, herring and cod liver oil. The action of sunlight on the skin is also a useful source of vitamin D. Children need vitamin D for the formation of healthy bones and teeth and children who are deficient in the vitamin are at risk of developing rickets. There has been a recent re-emergence of rickets amongst certain populations of children with darker skin, especially South Asian and African Caribbean children. Children with fair skin are likely to synthesize adequate levels of vitamin D through their skin, although in areas such as northern Scotland, where daylight hours are low in winter, fair-skinned children may also be at risk. For this reason the Chief Medical Officer for Health recommends that children under 5 years of age are given supplements of vitamin D (CMO, 2005).

Adequate levels of nutrition are also needed to optimize children's ability to learn. Research studies such as Glewwe et al. (2001) have demonstrated that better nourished children in the majority world perform better at school, partly due to children being well enough to start school at the usual age for school entry and partly due to improved health outcomes during their years at school, resulting in less 'lost' time.

The importance of children having an adequate breakfast before school is well documented. In a review of the literature, Papamandjaris (2000) concludes that eating an adequate breakfast before school has beneficial effects for children who are well nourished as well as those who are inadequately nourished. Previously well-nourished children who missed breakfast showed decreases in memory and problem-solving ability. Malnourished children who come to school hungry, show deficits in cognitive tests such as verbal fluency and arithmetic. In schools that operate a breakfast club, children are reported to concentrate better and academic performance is improved.

There have been many studies looking at the effects of **micronutrients** on children's behaviour and learning, with conclusions which give conflicting messages (Dani et al., 2005). Commercial interests have been quick to exploit parental insecurities about their children's diet and there are now a variety of products on the market designed to boost children's intelligence quotient (IQ) and school performance. The value of eating breakfast is even being used to promote the consumption of sugary breakfast cereals.

Dani et al. (2005: 258) have undertaken a literature review of available research in this area and conclude that nutrition has 'potent effects on brain function'. The authors consider that the consumption of breakfast, protein, iodine and iron all have an effect on children's behaviour and learning. In addition they conclude that, in certain behavioural disorders, such as **attention defici[t] hyperactivity disorder (ADHD)**, micronutrients such as essential fatty acids minerals and vitamins have an important role. The authors caution that w[e] need to await the results of large-scale trials before we reach conclusions as t[o] the benefits of routinely using supplements for children. However, it is cle[ar] that early years practitioners have a responsibility to take the nutrition of t[he] children they care for very seriously.

In July 2006 the Food Standards Agency published the result of a study conducted by Ellis et al., on the effects of diet on children's learning, education and school performance. The study, undertaken by the University of Teesside, looked at a variety of research projects which had published results on the effects of eating breakfast, short-term sugar intake on children with ADHD, fish oil supplements for children with symptoms of learning and behaviour disorder, and studies on vitamin and mineral supplementation. The researchers concluded that there are insufficient good quality research studies to come to any firm conclusions about the role of diet on children's learning for children in general. As in the Dani et al. (2005) review, it was recommended that there should be more studies in this area, using participants that are representative of the whole population, using universal, standardized measures and being of a longer duration. However, the research team did conclude that there was overwhelming evidence to suggest that physical activity, a diet low in fat and sugar, but high in fruits, vegetables and complex carbohydrates should be promoted for all children (Ellis et al., 2006).

Reflection point

If you are involved in an early years setting, examine the policies and procedures that set out the way your setting makes provision for children's food and eating. Do you think that provision reflects the prime importance of this area of care? What provision do you have for children who may not have had breakfast?

Food sensitivity

There is increasing concern about the numbers of children who demonstrate a degree of food sensitivity. Food sensitivity includes two different conditions, food allergy and food intolerance. Food allergy involves the immune system. If children eat something they are allergic to they may have a severe reaction which can be life-threatening. A food intolerance does not involve the immune system and generally symptoms are milder, but can still have adverse effects on a child's health and development (Food Standards Agency, 2006a; 2006b).

Food allergy

Most food allergy is acquired in the first two years of life, with 6 to 8 per cent of infants aged 1 year demonstrating a food allergy, falling until late childhood when a prevalence of 1 to 2 per cent is reported (Wood, 2003). The most commonly reported allergies are to milk, eggs, peanut butter, soy, wheat, shell-fish and some fruits and vegetables. As can be seen from the prevalence rates, some of these allergies are relatively short-lived, although some persist throughout adulthood. Symptoms of allergy include coughing, dry, itchy mouth and tongue, itchy rash, nausea, vomiting, diarrhoea, wheezing, shortness of breath, swelling of the lips and throat, runny or blocked nose, sore, red itchy eyes, faintness and collapse (Food Standards Agency, 2006a).

In 2001 a 5-month-old baby died whilst in the care of a private day nursery. The child's parents had informed the nursery that the baby was allergic to cow's milk, but, whilst in nursery, the child was given a breakfast cereal containing a cow's milk product (BBC, 2003).

Case study

Fiona has chosen Morning Star day nursery to care for her 2-year-old toddler when she returns to work full time. She is naturally anxious about leaving Chloe, especially as Chloe has been diagnosed with having a severe nut allergy. Chloe's mother has been given an **EpiPen** to use if Chloe begins to have an allergic reaction. Fiona can still remember the tragic case of the baby who died of an allergic reaction at nursery.

What measures should the staff at the Morning Star nursery take to ensure Chloe's safety in their care and to reassure Fiona that she can confidently leave her daughter with them?

The 'Allergy in schools' web site gives helpful information to help you with your planning: www.allergyinschools.org.uk/

Food allergies appear to be on the rise. This may be because we are more aware of the problem than before and previous figures may reflect a degree of under-diagnosis. However, there are studies that have shown that there is an underlying change. In particular, there appears to be a real increase in the number of cases of peanut allergy (Sicherer et al., 2003). In the following chapter we will be looking at guidelines aimed at reducing the incidence of food allergy in children.

Food intolerance

Food intolerance does not involve the immune system and generally symptoms do not occur as rapidly as with a food allergy and are not life-threatening. The most common foods that children are intolerant to are milk, lactose (milk sugar), gluten, wheat, food preservatives, red wine, cheese, chocolate and caffeine. Symptoms of food intolerance include: diarrhoea, weight loss, bloating, anaemia, flushing and migraine. (Food Standards Agency, 2006b).

Some children are intolerant to the gluten in wheat (Coeliac disease). These children may have symptoms of nausea, wind, tiredness, constipation, reduced growth and skin problems (Food Standards Agency, 2006b). It has been found that avoiding gluten during the weaning process reduces the incidence of Coeliac disease. This is discussed in the next chapter.

Food additives

When we prepare food at home we generally plan to eat the food in the next couple of days. We can extend the life of some foods by freezing or preserving (by using sugar to turn fruit into jam, or by using vinegar to pickle vegetables). Preprepared food that is sold in supermarkets often has to be stored and transported, so manufacturers use a number of substances to maintain the quality of the food and keep it safe to eat. Without many of these additives food would start to 'go off' due to microbial action. Additives include preservatives, colours and flavours.

Activity

Investigate the following web site. It will give you an excellent understanding of what is meant by a food additive.

www.understandingfoodadditives.org/index.htm (accessed 6 September 2007)

There has been growing concern that some of these additives could affect the health and behaviour of children. Van Bever et al. (1986) found that various additives including tartrazine, sodium benzoate, sodium glutamate and sodium metabisulphite had an adverse effect on children's eczema and, as early as 1975, Feingold proposed that food additives may influence the rate of hyperactivity in children (Stevenson, 2006). Following public concern, the Food Standards Agency (FSA) commissioned research by Stevenson to investigate further the effect of additives on children. The results of the study suggested that consumption of certain mixtures of artificial food colours and sodium benzoate preservative are associated with increases in hyperactive behaviour in children (FSA, 2007a). The Food Standards Agency, whilst recognizing that hyperactive behaviour in children can be influenced by factors such as genetics, prematurity, the child's environment and upbringing, advise parents of children who show signs of hyperactivity, or attention deficit hyperactivity disorder, to eliminate the colours used in the Stevenson study from the children's diet. These colours are:

▸ sunset yellow (E110)

▸ quinoline yellow (E104)

▸ carmoisine (E122)

▸ allura red (E129).

It seems sensible, therefore, for practitioners in early years settings to avoid giving children food that contains these colours. By law, any additives in food must be clearly displayed on the label, so it is a straightforward task to monitor this. However, particular care may need to be taken if food is brought into the setting by outside caterers.

Obesity

Incidence of childhood obesity

As a nation, **obesity** rates both for adults and for children are steadily rising, with the proportion who were categorized as obese (**body mass index** [BMI] over 30) increasing from 13.2 per cent of men in 1993 to 23.6 per cent in 2004 and from 16.4 per cent of women in 1993 to 23.8 per cent in 2004 (DoH, 2005). Among boys aged 2–10, between 1995 and 2004, there was an increase in the proportion that were obese, from 10 per cent to 16 per cent. There was a different pattern for girls aged 2–10, with no statistically significant increase in the rate of obesity, which remained at 12 per cent in 2004 (DoH, 2006a). The Millennium Cohort study that has followed a group of children since their birth at the start of the new millennium has found that at 3 years of age 18 per cent of children are already overweight and that 5 per cent are obese (Elliott, 2007).

Although, in adults, it is relatively straightforward to calculate an individual's body mass index, it is less straightforward for children. The adult calculation of weight divided by height squared, is inaccurate because children are still growing. Therefore, to measure obesity in children, special calculations are used which take account of the child's sex and age. The Health Survey of England uses the UK National BMI percentile classification (Jotangia et al., 2006).

Causes of childhood obesity

Previously in the chapter we looked at the three main macronutrients in our diet: fat, sugar and protein. We learned that these three substances supply the energy we need to grow and keep active. It was noted that if our diet supplies more energy than we need for growth and daily activity, the energy is stored as fat deposits in the body. Thus, the cause of childhood obesity is self-evident; these children are consuming diets that contain more energy than they need. However, this explanation does not explain why there has been such a rise in levels of adult and child obesity. Why is it that children are consuming more energy than they need? There is no simple answer; any explanation has to take account of a wide variety of influences including genetic factors, environmental factors, lifestyle preferences and the cultural environment of children (Dehghan et al., 2005).

> ▸ *Medical/genetic factors.* There are a few conditions that can cause weight gain in children, such as leptin deficiency, hypothyroidism and the side effects of drugs such as steroids (Dehghan et al., 2005).

> ▸ *Diet.* In recent years, food has become more affordable in the minority world. The emphasis placed on food has shifted from one of survival, to food choices becoming lifestyle choices. Whereas, in previous generations, food was cooked at home from basic ingredients, there is a shift to eating meals out of the home and buying pre-prepared foods that are higher in fat and sugar. In addition, there has been an increase in the consumption of drinks, carbonated or otherwise, that are full of sugar. The evidence that children are consuming more calories per day than they used to remains elusive, with some studies indicating that children are consuming fewer calories than in previous years (Dehghan et al., 2005). There is evidence that, within this, the proportion of saturated fat has risen, with 94 per cent of UK children aged 7–10 consuming more than the recommended amounts of saturated fat (BMA Board of Science, 2005).

> ▸ *Exercise.* It has been suggested that physical activity levels of children have reduced. There are many factors at work: a rise in the amount of television viewing and the playing of computer games, children being taken to school by car, less time spent on physical activities in school

and less opportunity for children to 'play out' after school. Research studies have confirmed that children who have low levels of physical activity are more at risk of becoming obese (Swinburn and Egger, 2002). Dehghan et al. (2005) report positive results for school-based interventions in the USA designed to promote higher activity levels in school children, both in taking more exercise, walking or cycling to school and reducing televion viewing. These interventions had a positive effect on the reduction of obesity levels. However a British Medical Association (BMA Board of Science, 2005) review of the literature suggests that increasing the level of activity of children in school had little effect on the overall activity levels of children.

The effects of obesity

The BMA Board of Science (2005: 7) identifies a number of health risks associated with children being obese and inactive.

▸ *Metabolic syndrome*. This is a cluster of conditions such as high blood pressure, high blood sugar and high cholesterol together with abdominal obesity which increases the risk of **cardiovascular disease** and type 2 **diabetes.** Early childhood obesity can lead to the development of this syndrome in later childhood and adulthood.

▸ *Type 2 diabetes*. This used to be a disease only seen in adults, but it is increasingly being seen in children. Once someone is diabetic there is an increasing risk that they may suffer cardiovascular disease, kidney failure, visual impairment and poor circulation leading to limb amputation.

▸ *Coronary heart disease*. Several studies have shown a link between weight gain in childhood and an increase in cardiovascular risk as adults. This connection is especially high in obese adults who were obese children.

▸ *Psychological difficulties*. Obese children are at increased risk of discrimination; and adolescents, girls especially, are less likely to be accepted into university, are less likely to form permanent relationships and are less likely to be 'economically well off' (Viner and Cole, 2005).

Obesity in both adults and children adds a significant burden to the National Health Service (NHS). The House of Commons Public Accounts Committee (HCPAC) calculated that obesity already costs about £1 billion a year with further indirect costs to the economy of £2.3 billion to £2.6 billion (HCPAC, 2007).

Preventative strategies to combat the rise in childhood obesity are discussed in Chapters 7 and 8.

Summary

▸ Nutrition can be looked at in two ways:

– the nutrient approach, which aims to quantify the nutrients we need for healthy growth and development
– the food group approach, which aims to identify the different types of foods we need to supply the nutrients we need.

▸ Nutrients can be divided into macronutrients, that is, carbohydrates, proteins and fats, and micronutrients, that is, vitamins and minerals. Water and fibre are also needed for healthy growth and development.

▸ The five main food groups are: bread, cereals and potatoes; fuit and vegetables; milk and dairy products; meat, fish and vegetable alternatives; and foods containing fats and sugars.

▸ A diet deficient in nutrients can lead to ill health. Conditions related to a poor diet include, under-nutrition, obesity, oral disease, iron deficiency anaemia and vitamin D deficiency. Inadequate nutrition can have negative effects on learning and possibly on behaviour.

▸ Some children may have a food allergy or food intolerance that may cause illness.

▸ Obesity in children is rising; children are consuming more energy than they need. Causes may include medical or genetic conditions, a change to foods higher in fat and sugar than in previous generations, and a reduction in the amount of exercise taken.

▸ Obesity can lead to metabolic syndrome, type 2 diabetes, coronary heart disease and psychological difficulties.

Discussion points

▸ At the moment there is no conclusive evidence about the effectiveness of nutritional supplements on children's learning. Should we routinely give supplements to well-nourished children just to be on the safe side?

▸ Obesity in children is rising, and preventative measures have to be taken to protect children from becoming overweight. Should the blame be laid at the feet of parents?

Further reading

Dani, J., Burrill, C. and Demmig-Adams, B.(2005) 'The remarkable role of nutrition on learning and behaviour', *Nutrition and Food Science*, 35(4): 258–63.

James, W. (2006) 'The challenge of childhood obesity', *International Journal of Paediatric Obesity*, 1: 7–10. www.iotf.org/documents/IOTFIJPOpapers.pdf (accessed 25 July 2007).

Useful web sites

The British Nutrition Foundation www.nutrition.org.uk/ has a good section on the important nutrients in our diet (accessed 25 July 2007).

The Department of Health has a good section on obesity with links to childhood obesity:

www.dh.gov.uk/PolicyAndGuidance/HealthAndSocialCareTopics/Obesity/fs/en (accessed 25 July 2007).

The Food Standards web site has relevant sections on the effects of food on children's health, behaviour and learning, including good resources on allergies and food intolerances: www.food.gov.uk/ (accessed 25 July 2007).

Healthy Eating Guidelines

In Chapter 2 we looked at the role that nutrition plays in human health and development. In this chapter we look at current guidelines for the best way of ensuring that our diets contain the necessary nutrients we need in the correct proportions. The first part of this chapter looks at healthy eating guidelines for adults, then we look at nutritional guidelines for pre-conception, pregnancy, infancy and the under 5s and children aged 5-8 years. Guidelines directed specifically for early years settings and school settings are discussed in detail.

In some early years settings, children attend for the majority of their waking hours, for most of the weeks in the year, so we have an immense responsibility to ensure that the meals we provide are of high quality. In addition, we need to have an understanding of the latest recommendations for healthy eating during pregnancy, as we may be in a position where mothers seek our advice. Working with children is very demanding; children and parents rely on us to be fit and well, so the chapter starts with an investigation into the kinds of foods we should be eating to keep us healthy. As with the last chapter, an empirical, scientific approach will be taken, the guidelines being based on up-to-date research.

The key areas that are covered in this chapter are:

▸ Healthy eating guidelines for adults

▸ Healthy eating guidelines for conception and pregnancy

▸ Providing food and drink for infants 0–1 year

▸ Providing food and drink for children 1–5 years (nursery guidelines)

▸ Providing food and drink for children 5–8 years (school guidelines).

Healthy eating guidelines for adults

It is only comparatively recently that governments in the minority world have become concerned about the ill effects of the diet that we are eating. Up until the Second World War the emphasis was on trying to ensure that the population had sufficient calories. You will recall that in Chapter 1 we looked at the introduction of food rationing; ironically, in the UK, the nation's health improved during the time of war rationing since people living in poverty actually received a better diet than they were eating before (British Nursing News On Line, 2006).

Activity

Investigate this site, it has interesting material on food rationing. Why do you think that the nation's health improved on the wartime ration?

www.worldwar2exraf.co.uk/Online%20Museum/Museum%20Docs/ foodration.html (accessed 25 July 2007).

Trying to make sense of all the nutritional information that comes our way is very difficult and, at times, confusing. There is not a day passes without an item about an aspect of nutrition being debated on television or in the newspapers. If we look at the Internet there are many hundreds of web sites that give information, some of which is out of date or has no scientific validity. As individuals, it is almost impossible to make conclusions about what constitutes a 'healthy diet'. One example is the status of butter in our diet. It used to be thought that butter was 'bad' for you as it was believed that it contributed to raised serum choles- terol in the body. Many people switched to margarine, in an effort to reduce risk. Later research has indicated that margarine can be equally unhealthy, so con- sumers have been left confused and distrustful of health advice.

The UK government has the promotion of a healthy diet and lifestyle high on its agenda and has endeavoured to translate the recommendations from a wide vari- ety of professionals into a user-friendly set of guidelines. This is not easy as it involves collaboration between nutritionalists, epidemiologists, psychologists, educators, professional communicators, medical doctors, industrialists and legis- lators' (Marks et al., 2005: 131). In an effort to synthesize advice from such a vari- ety of sources, the government set up the Committee on Medical Aspects of Food and Nutrition Policy in 1963 (FSA, 2001). In 1991 COMA published an estimation of nutritional requirements for different groups within the population, which are:

- ▶ Boys and girls (aged 0–3 months; 4–6 months; 7–9 months; 10–12 months; 1–3 years; 4–6 years; 7–10 years)

- ▶ Males (aged 11–14 years; 15–18 years; 19–50 years; 50+ years)

- ▶ Females (aged 11–14 years; 15–18 years; 19–50 years; 50+ years; pregnancy and breastfeeding). (BNF, 2007)

The eatwell plate

Use the eatwell plate to help you get the balance right. It shows how
much of what you eat should come from each food group.

Figure 3.1   The Eatwell Plate

© The Eatwell Plate, The Food Standards Agency, www.food.gov.uk, 17 September 2007

The Committee on Medical Aspects of Food and Nutrition Policy set out their recommendations in terms of **Dietary reference values** for the amount of energy and nutrients in our diet. Since then, COMA has been superseded by the Scientific Advisory Committee on Nutrition (SACN). This is a committee of independent experts that advises the Food Standards Agency and the Department of Health about the diet and nutritional status of the population as well as giving advice about the nutritional content of individual foods.

It is not enough for committees such as COMA and SACN to produce scientific advice and recommendations. To effect behavioural change, any message about healthy eating has to be 'simple, clear and consistent' (Marks et al., 2005: 130). To help us to understand recommendations about healthy eating more clearly, a number of pictorial devices have been used. In the UK, healthy eating guidelines include different types of foods that are recommended. The Eatwell Plate, as the representation is called, applies to most healthy people over the age of 2. It does not apply to children under 2 because they need full fat milk and dairy products. Between the ages of 2 and 5 children should make a gradual transition to family foods, and the recommended balance shown in the Eatwell Plate (Figure 3.1) can begin to apply.

In the USA the guidelines have been represented in the form of a pyramid. The US Department of Agriculture (USDA) is committed to updating this every five years, the latest version having been published in 2005. There is a degree of controversy over the production of the USDA pyramid. The Harvard School of

Public Health (2006) considers that it does not contain sufficient information to help individuals make informed choices and actually recommends foods that are not essential for health.

Activity

Investigate the web sites below that are devoted to giving information about healthy eating.

1 Make a comparison between each set of recommendations. Do you think it 'matters' that there are so many differences or does it, perhaps, just reflect the ever changing field of knowledge about nutrition?

2 How useful do you think the interactive web sites are?

3 Note the resources that you could use with children.

4 The web sites listed below are for the UK and USA. Investigate guidelines for other countries (the information is easily available on the Internet). Are the messages similar?

www.eatwell.gov.uk/healthydiet/eatwellplate/ (The Eatwell Plate)

www.eatwell.gov.uk/(UK healthy eating guidelines from the Food Standards Agency)

www.mypyramid.gov/ (the USDA home page for their pyramid)

www.mypyramidtracker.gov/ (an interactive site to help you assess how your diet and exercise levels compare with the USDA recommendations)

www.hsph.harvard.edu/nutritionsource/pyramids.html (Harvard School of Public Health).

(All web sites accessed 27 July 2007)

The UK government's guidelines for a healthy diet for adults

The Eatwell Plate model reflects findings that a 'Mediterranean'-type diet protects against diet-related diseases such as diabetes and coronary heart disease. The diet contains a high proportion of vegetables, fruit and cereal, a moderate to high intake of fish, a low intake of saturated fat, but an increased consumption of unsaturated oils such as olive oil, a low to moderate intake of dairy products and a low consumption of sugar (Trichopoulou, 2005).

The plate is shown divided into sections, each section representing a particular food group. The size of the section reflects the proportion of that particular food group needed in your overall diet. Together with the visual representation there are additional guidelines to help individuals plan their diet.

> ▶ *Enjoy your food.* Relax while you are eating and make food a sociable occasion as often as possible.

> ▶ *Eat a variety of foods.* No single food will supply all the nutrients needed to keep you healthy. Include some of your favourite foods from time to time even if they are not especially 'healthy'. The Eatwell Plate suggests that one-third of a meal should contain complex carbohydrates such as bread, other cereals and potatoes. A third should consist of fruit and vegetables, with the other third divided between meat, fish and alternatives and dairy products. Foods containing fats, oils and sugars should be eaten sparingly.

> ▶ *Eat the right amount to be a healthy weight.* Food contains energy which the body uses to keep active. People who lead very physically active lives need to eat more than people who are inactive. The amount of energy you need also depends upon your size, so a petite woman will need less food than a 6-foot tall man, but children who are growing need proportionately more food than their size alone would predict. Whatever your energy needs, the proportions of food from the five food groups should remain the same.

> ▶ *Eat plenty of food rich in starch and fibre,* such as rice, potatoes, bread, pasta and other cereals. Choose wholegrain cereal foods wherever possible.

> ▶ *Eat plenty of fruit and vegetables, at least five portions a day.* There is evidence that this reduces the risk of diseases such as coronary heart disease and some cancers.

> ▶ *Do not eat too many foods that contain a lot of fat.* Fat is high in calories and eating too much can lead to becoming overweight, however we all need some fat in our diet. As well as trimming visible fat from food before cooking it is wise to reduce consumption of foods like pies, pastries, cakes, biscuits and meat products such as sausages and burgers that contain 'hidden fat'. Some fats and oils, such as olive oil and oily fish, are beneficial and these should remain part of our diet.

> ▶ *Do not have sugary foods and drinks too often.* Too much sugar can contribute to dental disease and being overweight, so these foods should only be eaten occasionally.

> ▶ *Do not eat too many foods high in salt* and cut down on the amount of salt added in cooking and at the table. Eating too much salt can lead to high blood pressure. Manufactured food is often very high in salt.

▸ *Eat moderate amounts of dairy products,* such as milk, cheese and yoghurt. These foods are rich in calcium, vitamins and protein. Wherever possible eat the low fat versions. (Wired for Health, 2007).

The Eatwell Plate was introduced in 2007. The guidelines have been simplified into eight tips for healthy eating.

1   Base your meals on starchy foods.

2   Eat lots of fruit and vegetables.

3   Eat more fish.

4   Cut down on saturated fat and sugar

5   Try to eat less salt, no more than 6 g a day

6   Get active and try to be a healthy weight.

7   Drink plenty of water.

8   Do not skip breakfast. (Food Standard Agency, 2007b)

Reflection point

In the preceding section we have investigated a variety of approaches to giving people information and guidance about how to eat healthily. We have seen how information changes over time and between different countries. Do you think that the information is 'simple, clear and consistent' (Marks et al., 2005)?

The Food Standards Agency has introduced a food labelling system based on traffic lights to inform consumers about the relative amounts of fat, saturates, sugar and salt in food products. Many manufacturers have decided to use a different system based on guideline daily amounts of calories, sugar, fats, saturates and salts in products. Do you think it matters that there are two different approaches to food labelling? www. eatwell.gov.uk/foodlabels/ understandlabels/ provides an explanation of food labelling from the FSA web site (accessed 25 July 2007).

Healthy eating guidelines for conception and pregnancy

The nutritional status of women of childbearing age has an important effect on:

▸ the ability to conceive

▸ the health of the unborn child

▸ the incidence of premature births and babies who are small for dates

▸ the subsequent health of the baby

▸ the health of the offspring in adulthood.

Pre-conception

There is a proven link between nutritional status, the ability to conceive and early miscarriage. Women who are obese (BMI over 30) are more likely to have irregular menstrual cycles and a greater risk of infertility than women of normal body weight. In addition, once pregnant they are more likely to miscarry. (American Society for Reproductive Medicine, 2001). The relationship between obesity and the risk of infertility has also been noted in men. Men who are obese have lower sperm counts and may experience hormonal changes that have a negative effect on conception (Markku et al., 2006). Low body weight also has a negative effect on a woman's ability to conceive. Women who have very low levels of body fat often menstruate irregularly or not at all.

Being obese or underweight around the time of conception can also have an effect on the growing baby. Women who are underweight have a higher risk of babies who are premature or 'small for dates' (Jackson and Robinson, 2001). In addition, underweight women are more likely to be deficient in micronutrients which may have an adverse effect on foetal development. Babies of women, who are obese at the time of conception, are also at risk of poor foetal growth (Jackson and Robinson, 2001).

Healthy eating during preconception

The recommendations for healthy eating around this time are similar to the general recommendations for a healthy diet for adults. It is important that as well as being the right height for weight, women take care to eat foods that are rich in the following:

▸ *Iron*. Iron is essential for the production of red blood cells. During pregnancy a woman's need for iron increases as she has more blood in her system and she also has to supply the baby with sufficient iron for its developing blood system. Insufficient iron can lead to increased risks of prematurity and **perinatal mortality** (Jackson and Robinson, 2001). In addition, the mother may lose blood during the birth so she has to have sufficient stores of iron to prevent her from becoming anaemic after her confinement. Iron can be found in red meat, pulses, dried fruit, bread, green vegetables and fortified breakfast cereals. Eating foods rich in vitamin C, whilst eating foods containing iron, helps the body make best use of the iron in food.

▸ *Calcium*. Calcium is found in dairy products such as milk and cheese. It can also be found in green leafy vegetables (such as broccoli, cabbage and okra, but not spinach), soya beans, tofu, soya drinks with added calcium, nuts, bread and anything made with fortified flour, and fish where you eat the bones. Adequate levels of calcium protect against high blood pressure during pregnancy and may be needed for the formation of the baby's bones. Calcium is present in breast milk, so mothers who breastfeed need adequate levels of calcium. Women are at risk of losing calcium from their bones if there is not sufficient calcium in their diet (O'Brien et al., 2006).

▸ *Folic acid*. Foods rich in folates (the natural form of folic acid) are recommended. These include fortified breakfast cereals and bread, green vegetables and brown rice. Folic acid supplementation (400 micrograms daily) is recommended by the UK government from the time contraception is stopped until the twelfth week of pregnancy (FSA, 2007b). Folic acid supplementation can protect against the risk of a child being born with a **neural tube** defect such as spina bifida. The neural tube is formed in the very earliest stage of pregnancy, often when a woman is unaware that she is carrying a baby. Starting supplements before conception is the best way to protect the foetus. Folic acid supplementation also reduces the risk of a mother having a low birth weight baby (Jackson and Robinson, 2001).

There are certain foods that women planning to have a child should avoid.

▸ *Foods rich in vitamin A*. The government recommends that during preconception and pregnancy women should avoid eating liver and liver pâté. Vitamin supplements containing vitamin A should also be avoided. Too much vitamin A has been linked to babies being born with abnormalities.

▸ *Eat no more than two portions of oily fish a week*. Shark, swordfish and marlin should be avoided altogether and the amount of tuna should be limited. The UK government recommends a limit of two tuna steaks or four medium cans of tuna a week. There is evidence that the high levels of mercury in the fish could harm the nervous system of the developing baby (FSA, 2007b).

▸ *Alcohol should be avoided completely*. Women who choose to drink are advised to keep to a maximum of one or two units of alcohol once or twice a week (DoH, 2007b).

▸ *Peanuts.* Some people have food allergies, or other 'allergic' conditions such as asthma, hay fever and eczema. These **atopic** conditions have a genetic component and it has been found that if women with these conditions avoid eating peanuts during preconception and pregnancy, the risk that their children will develop a food allergy to peanuts is reduced.

Reflection point

Guidelines about what women should eat when planning a pregnancy change frequently. However very many babies are unplanned and mothers will not have had the opportunity to consciously put these recommendations into practice.

▸ Do you think that all fertile women should take folic acid supplements?

▸ What about alcohol? What implications are there for social drinking?

Healthy eating during pregnancy

The dietary recommendations for women, once they are pregnant, are very similar to the guidelines issued for all adults and are based on the Eatwell Plate model. As for women planning to conceive, there are an emphasis on being the right weight for height. There is an increasing amount of evidence that being overweight in pregnancy has detrimental effects for both mother and child. Mothers who are obese during pregnancy are at significantly increased risk of complications during pregnancy and have a greater risk of stillbirth (Sebire et al., 2001). Obesity in mothers has also been related to a 30–40 per cent increase in the chance of giving birth to a baby with major birth defects (Deckelbaum, 2002).

In a review of the literature, King (2006) outlined the following as being possible effects of obesity during pregnancy:

▸ increased risk of neural tube defects and congenital abnormalities

▸ increased risk of **pre-eclampsia**

▸ alteration in the way glucose is metabolised by the mother leading to the foetus receiving excessive levels of energy rich nutrients including glucose, lipids and amino acids. This can lead to the baby being born large for dates, which can lead to health problems

Being underweight also has significant risks to the foetus, as there is an increased risk of the baby being born early or small for date (Centres for Disease Control and Prevention, 2005). Teenagers are at particular risk of entering pregnancy underweight and they need special monitoring. Moran (2007), in a review of the literature, concluded that adolescents tended to have diets that were significantly deficient in energy, iron, folate, calcium, vitamin E and magnesium.

Advice for pregnant women about specific nutrients needed in pregnancy is similar to recommendations for preconception. The advice for iron, calcium and folic acid remains the same. In addition, women are advised to eat foods rich in vitamin D as it helps the body use the calcium in their diet. We get most of our vitamin D through the action of sunlight on our skins. Women with dark skins, especially Asian women, are at particular risk of vitamin D deficiency. There are very few foods that contain vitamin D, but it is found in eggs and oily fish. It is also added to some foods such as margarine, bread, breakfast cereals and powdered milk. Because of the difficulty in getting sufficient vitamin D from the diet, the government recommends that pregnant women take a supplement of 10 mcg of vitamin D each day (FSA, 2007b).

The foetus is vulnerable to infections that cross the placenta barrier from mother to baby. Because of this vulnerability, pregnant women have to be careful to avoid certain foods that may carry infections. These include:

▸ *soft cheeses* such as Camembert and Brie, or any other cheese that has a similar rind. 'Blue' cheeses such as Stilton should also be avoided as they contain a kind of mould. These cheeses could also carry the listeria bacteria, which could harm the baby

▸ *any type of pâté* which could carry listeria

▸ *raw or partially cooked eggs* that may carry the bacteria salmonella. (Cooking kills the bacteria)

▸ *raw or undercooked meat*, especially poultry and meat cooked on a barbecue which may not be cooked through.

▸ *undercooked ready meals*

▸ *raw shellfish*.

In addition to foods that may cause illness, there are foods that should be avoided for other reasons:

▸ *Foods containing high levels of vitamin A*, and some types of fish and alcohol. The advice is the same as for preconception.

▸ *Peanuts*. The advice is the same as for preconception.

▸ *Caffeine* should be limited to 300 mg a day as it has been linked with miscarriage and low birth weight. Caffeine is found in tea, coffee and chocolate, and some 'energy' drinks. Three mugs of instant coffee contain 300 mg of caffeine, as do six cups of tea.

Activity

Investigate these two web sites that will give you information about diet and nutrition in pregnancy.

www.dh.gov.uk/en/Publicationsandstatistics/Publications/Publications PolicyAndGuidance/DH_074920 The Department of Health issues *The Pregnancy Book* each year. This is the 2007 version.
www.hebs.scot.nhs.uk/readysteadybaby/index.htm This is the Health Education Board for Scotland's web site called 'Ready, Steady Baby'

(Both accessed 25 July 2007.)

Providing food and drink for infants 0–1 year

The natural food for human infants is breast milk; however in the first four months of life only 35 per cent of infants worldwide are being exclusively breastfed (World Health Organization, 2003). In the UK the majority of mothers (78 per cent in England) commence breastfeeding, but the rate drops to 48 per cent after six weeks and by six months only 25 per cent of babies are being breastfed. However these figures include mothers who supplement feeds with bottle feeds and/or have introduced other foods into the babies' diets. If one looks at the numbers of mothers who exclusively breastfeed the percentage drops to 22 per cent at six weeks and 8 per cent at four months in England. By six months the rate of exclusive breast feeding is negligible (Information Centre for Health and Social Care, 2007).

According to figures from WHO, inappropriate feeding practices are responsible for nearly two-thirds of the approximately 11 million deaths of children under 5 each year. The main concerns are that:

> complementary feeding (weaning on to foods other than breast milk) begins too early or too late

> foods are often nutritionally inadequate or unsafe

> malnourished children who survive often suffer lifelong illness/impaired development

> inappropriate feeding practices can lead to obesity

> poor feeding practices are a major threat to social and economic development.

▸ maternal and infant health and nutritional status are interlinked, so improved infant nutrition begins with initiatives to improve women's nutrition throughout all stages of their lives (WHO, 2003: 5).

The World Health Organization and UNICEF undertook a two-year process to look at scientific evidence and epidemiological evidence about feeding infants and young children. They published a global strategy (WHO, 2003) intended as a guide to action, for governments and concerned organizations, outlining a number of interventions designed to improve infant nutrition. These interventions and recommendations include:

▸ the development and implementation of policies on infant feeding by all governments

▸ recommendation that mothers should breastfeed exclusively for six months, and then continue breastfeeding up until the child is 2 years of age, whilst introducing adequate and safe complementary food.

▸ an expectation that health workers should give effective counselling, making use of trained lay or peer counsellors to extend this service into the community.

▸ an expectation that governments should review their progress on implementing the International Code of Marketing Breast Milk Substitutes.

▸ an expectation that governments should put legislation in place to protect the breastfeeding rights of working women (WHO, 2003).

Reflection point

Why do you think that a global strategy is needed? Should we be concentrating our efforts in parts of the world where malnutrition and poverty have a more profound effect than in Europe and the UK? These web sites may help you come to a conclusion.

www.unhchr.ch/html/menu3/b/k2crc.htm This is the link to the WHO's *Global Strategy for Infant and Young Child Feeding*.

www.who.int/nutrition/publications/code_english.pdf The link to the *International Code of Marketing Breast Milk Substitutes*.

www.unhchr.ch/html/menu3/b/k2crc.htm This is the web site for the Convention on the Rights of the Child. Are there any articles that could relate to this?

(All accessed 25 July 2007.)

The benefits of breastfeeding

Breast milk is a dynamic substance that changes in composition according to the age of the baby; so that the milk a mother produces when her baby is new-born is different from the milk produced six months later. In addition, the composition of breast milk changes during a feed so that for the first part of a feed the baby is getting a less dense fore milk that satisfies thirst, whilst the hind milk is richer and satisfies hunger. As well as all the nutrients that a baby needs, breast milk carries some of the mother's antibodies so the baby receives passive protection from infections. (British Nutrition Foundation, 2007)

The United Nations Children's Fund (2006) undertook a review of the literature and summarized the benefits of breastfeeding for infants' health and development as follows:

▸ Artificially fed babies are at greater risk of infections such as gastro-enteritis, respiratory infections, necrotizing enterocolitis, urinary tract infections and ear infections. Artificially fed babies are also more likely to have allergic conditions and to have insulin-dependent diabetes.

▸ Breastfed babies may have better neurological/cognitive development.

▸ Breastfed babies are less likely to be obese or to suffer cardiovascular disease in later life.

▸ Breastfed babies may be at less risk of childhood cancers and of sudden infant death syndrome (although babies who share a bed with parents may be more at risk).

▸ Breastfed babies may have better dental health (less dental disease and better alignment of teeth).

▸ There is some evidence to suggest that breastfeeding may lower the risk of multiple sclerosis, acute appendicitis and tonsillectomy.

For the mother, breastfeeding may be protective against breast cancer, ovarian cancer, hip fractures and low bone density. There is some suggestion that mothers who breastfeed have a reduced risk of rheumatoid arthritis. Breastfeeding also has the advantage of helping a mother regain her figure, as the fat stored during pregnancy is used in the formation of milk for the baby (UNICEF, 2006).

In mothers who are HIV positive, there is a risk that their babies can become infected through the breast milk. In the UK, the advice is that mothers who are HIV positive should not breastfeed, but should use artificial feeding instead. The risk to babies' health associated with artificial feeding is less than the risk of acquiring the HIV virus (DoH, 2004a). However, in the conditions of extreme poverty and poor hygiene that exist in much of the majority world, it is recognized that the risk to the baby of artificial feeding is higher than the risk of breastfeeding. In many areas of the world, artificial feeding is associated with devastatingly high rates of infant death due to malnutrition and gastro-intestinal disease. The World Health Organization (2006) has formulated new guidelines based on recent research evidence.

▸   Mothers who are HIV positive should breastfeed exclusively for the first six months of the baby's life, unless replacement feeding is 'acceptable, feasible, affordable, sustainable and safe' (WHO, 2006: 4).

▸   Once the baby reaches 6 months of age, 'if replacement feeding still does not meet the AFASS criteria, continued breastfeeding with comple-mentary feeding is recommended while the baby is continually assessed' (WHO, 2006: 4)

Of course, few mothers make the choice to breastfeed just on the possible health benefits to the child. There are a great many other factors that influence their decision.

Reflection point

Are you a parent? How did you feed your child/children? What factors did you take into consideration when deciding what method to use? If possible ask others about their experiences. Try to talk to parents who were brought up in another country or who are from a different socio-economic group than you.

Factors such as a mother's socio-economic group and ethnicity, have been found to have a significant effect on her decision to breastfeed and when to introduce the child to other foods. Breastfeeding rates in the UK are higher in the higher socio-economic groups (Wright et al., 2004) and among black and Asian mothers (Kelly et al., 2006). Within the UK as a whole, initial breastfeed-ing rates are higher in England (78 per cent) than in Scotland (70 per cent), with 67 per cent of mothers initially breastfeeding their children in Wales and 63 per cent in Northern Ireland (Information Centre for Health and Social Care, 2007). However, as we shall see when we look at when mothers introduce foods other than breast milk into babies' diets, these figures indicating the percentages of mothers breastfeeding at birth are misleading. In the UK very few babies are breastfed exclusively until the recommended age of 6 months.

Other factors such as cost, convenience, the wishes of the family, mother's health and employment status all influence maternal decisions. Our society has ambiva-lent attitudes towards the female breast. On the one hand, biologically the breast's function is to produce breast milk to feed infants. On the other hand the breast is linked to our feelings of sexuality. Mothers who wish to breastfeed outside the privacy of their home are sometimes faced with negative attitudes from others. We look at the issue of culture and identity in more detail in Chapter 6.

There are various government initiatives to encourage mothers to breastfeed. In 2003, the government set a target to increase the numbers of mothers initiating breastfeeding by 2 per cent a year. The latest figures from the 2005 Infant Feeding Survey seem to suggest that there has been an improvement since the 2002 survey.

Activity

Conduct an Internet search. What government initiatives can you find that encourage breastfeeding in England, Scotland, Wales and Northern Ireland?

What other organizations are active in this field? Looking back at the recommendations of the WHO (2003), *Global Strategy for Infant Feeding and Young Child Feeding*, as previously outlined in this chapter, to what extent do you think these recommendations have been implemented in the UK?

What advice about diet does the 'Eatwell' web site give to breastfeeding mothers?

As with the decision to start breastfeeding, the decision as to when to stop is also influenced by a whole raft of different factors. We have seen that the WHO recommends that breastfeeding continues until the child is 2 years of age. However, in the UK there are very few mothers who breastfeed for that long. The current advice (DoH, 2007c) is that mothers should try to continue breast-feeding until the child is 1 year old, but can continue as long as they want. There is some suggestion that prolonged breastfeeding is a risk for cardiovas-cular disease later in life (Martin et al., 2005) but the evidence is unclear and the advice to mothers remains the same.

Mothers who continue to breastfeed their children beyond the age of 2 are often met with disapproval from others. This is a cultural phenomenon; in many coun-tries children are breastfed until the next child is born and the last child may be breastfed for over three years. For instance in Bangladesh and West Bengal the median duration of breastfeeding is 36 months (Ramachandran, 2004).

Bottle-feeding

We have seen that the guidelines for infant feeding are that babies should be exclusively breastfed until they are 6 months old. Therefore, in an ideal world, the only time a baby should be bottle-fed is when the mother expresses her milk to enable the baby to be fed by someone else, or health reasons prevent the mother from breastfeeding. We have also seen that, at the moment, in the UK, the number of mothers who exclusively breastfeed for six months is negligible.

This poses a dilemma for those of us working with mothers of young babies. It is our responsibility to promote breastfeeding, whilst at the same time respecting the decision of the parents. We have seen the very many reasons why a mother may decide to bottle-feed, and to be too negative could harm the relationship we have with the mother. For some mothers, it is necessary that they go out to work and the baby will be looked after by someone else. Thus, many early years practitioners will need to know how to bottle-feed infants, and to prepare and store feeds in such a way that the children's health is not compromised.

Artificial milk is based on cow's milk that has been modified to bring its composition as close to human breast milk as possible. Babies less than 1 year of age should not be given unmodified cow's milk as the protein level is too high and it could damage their kidneys. The fatty acids in human breast milk are needed for human brain development, and human breast milk contains all the other substances, some known, some unknown, that are needed for human growth.

There are a number of baby milk formulas on the market. They can be divided into formulas designed for infants from birth and follow-on milks designed for older, hungrier babies. Although there has been promotion of 'progress' milks or 'follow-on milks' for older babies, there is no evidence to suggest that these have advantages over other milks (GOSHT, 2007). Some children are allergic to, or have intolerance to, formula milk based on cow's milk. Before swapping to a non-cow's milk-based formula, parents need advice from their health-care professional (midwife, health visitor or general practitioner [GP]). Previously some children may have been swapped to formulas based on goat's milk. Since March 2007 infant formulas based on goat's milk have not been sold in the UK as they are not thought to be suitable for children under 1 year of age, and children who cannot tolerate cow's milk are unlikely to tolerate goat's milk either (DoH, 2007a). Milks based on soya should only be used on the advice of health professionals as introducing soya into infants' diets too early has been linked to food allergies later on in life (FSA, 2007b).

It is important that all those professionally involved with the care of infants, who are required to give bottle-feeds, are properly trained. Early years settings should have policies and procedures in place that ensure the safe preparation and storage of feeds within the setting, or procedures in place for the hygienic storage of feeds brought in from home.

Introducing children to foods other than milk

By the time babies are 6 months old, a diet exclusively of breast milk will no longer be adequate for optimum growth. By 6 months, babies can be expected to have more than doubled their birth weight and a milk-only diet will be deficient in iron, vitamins A and D and energy (Thurtle, 1998). The time is right to start the weaning process because:

- by 6 months, babies are physiologically mature enough to process the additional amounts of protein

- babies are able to hold objects and bring them to their mouths

- babies' mouths are very sensitive and are used as an important way to learn about the world around them

- at this age babies will be able to swallow a mouthful of food

- babies are curious and will probably already have been reaching out and touching their parents' food. They will have been getting used to different tastes

- babies seem to be receptive to different tastes and textures at this age; left much later and babies may start to reject the weaning process

- moving on to other foods helps babies develop the ability to chew, which seems to be important in learning to speak (Thurtle, 1998).

The decision about when to wean and what foods to introduce, is influenced by many factors. Although the guidelines are specific about timing, as with the choice between breast and bottle, there is a difference between what health professionals recommend and what parents decide to do. In 2004, Wright et al. discovered that despite recommendations that weaning should not start before 6 months, the average age weaning commenced was 3.5 months. Twenty-one per cent of children had been introduced to different foods by 3 months and only 6 per cent had been older than 4 months. In the study, most parents said that guidelines given by health professionals were not important in their decision when to start weaning. The most powerful influence appeared to be rapid weight gain of the baby in the first six weeks of life with parents perceiving that the baby was hungry. Mothers from lower socio-economic groups started weaning earlier.

If health professionals are not influencing the decision of parents then who is? Thurtle (1998) suggests that the family kinship group is the most powerful influence, with mothers taking advice from their mothers and other relatives. Religious practices and the families' own eating practices also influence the decision about when to wean and what foods to offer.

Current guidelines in the UK are that, between 6 months and 1 year old, babies should be gradually weaned from an exclusively milk diet to one where solid food is the main part of the diet. There is recognition that all babies are different and that the rate of transition will be variable. During these six months the texture of the food offered will change from being sloppy enough to be sucked off a spoon to being mashed and chopped. In addition to the gradual introduction of different foods, it is advisable for parents to give children between the ages of 6 months to 5 years old vitamin drops containing vitamins A, C and D. The following guidelines have been taken from the Eatwell web site (FSA, 2007b).

Stage 1

▸ Suggestions for first weaning foods are puréed vegetables, fruit and cereal.

▸ First tastes should be mixed with a little breast or formula milk (not cow's milk as this should be avoided until the child is 1 year old).

▸ Wheat-based foods and nuts and seeds, eggs and shellfish should not be given to children in the initial stages of weaning.

▸ In the early stages babies will still be getting the majority of their nutrition from breast or formula milk (about 500 to 600 ml a day).

Stage 2

▸ Gradually the amount of solid food will increase so that solid food is introduced at two and then three meals a day, but milk should still remain an important part of babies' diets (500 to 600 ml a day).

▸ Cereals should be given just once a day.

▸ No salt, sugar or honey should be added.

▸ Gradually foods such as purées of meat or poultry can be added, as well as pulses such as lentils.

▸ Full fat milk products can be introduced such as yoghurt and fromage frais. Full fat milk can be used in cooking, but not as a drink.

Stage 3

▸ The baby can be introduced to a wider variety of different foods, whilst still having 500 to 600 ml of milk daily.

▸ Two or three servings of starchy food such as potatoes, bread or rice should be given together with fruit and vegetables for at least two meals.

▸ Soft cooked meat, fish, egg (well cooked) and tofu can be introduced.

▸ Foods can be lumpier in texture and finger foods such as pitta bread, bananas and carrot sticks can be introduced. It is important to monitor babies during feeding to make sure that they do not choke.

Stage 4

▸ At this stage babies are fitting into family meals and are eating three minced or chopped meals a day, whilst still consuming 500–600 ml of milk as the main drink.

▸ Three to four servings of starchy foods and fruits and vegetables are recommended.

▸ If children are not being given meat, then protein-rich vegetarian food should be given, such as peas, beans and lentils.

▸ Babies have small stomachs and need full fat milk products to ensure that they get enough energy.

▸ Healthy snacks of fruit, pitta bread or cheese can be given if the child is hungry.

▸ Avoid salt, sugar and honey

▸ Drinks should be restricted to milk, water and diluted fruit juice (from 6 months). Tea, coffee and diet drinks should not be given to young children. The use of fruit squashes, fizzy drinks and flavoured milk is not recommended, but if used they should be restricted to meal-times and should be diluted.

Providing food and drink for children 1–5 years (nursery guidelines)

From 1 year of age children should be eating 'family meals'. However, there are some fundamental differences between the nutrient requirements of the under 5 and older children and adults. There have been incidents when caring adults have thought that they were providing the best possible nutrition for their child by adhering to the healthy eating guidelines for adults. As a result there have been cases of malnutrition.

Reflection point

We have been using the term 'family meals' within the discussion about weaning. What do you think this means in today's society? Within the nursery setting children and early years practitioners tend to sit down together at regular times of the day for meals. Is this the experience of the majority of the children you care for when they are at home? If you have a family, is this what happens in your house? Is a regular time when everyone gets together to eat of nutritional importance, or is it a cultural phenomenon? How many of our childcare practices around feeding/weaning are to do with culture and tradition?

Young children are growing fast and require proportionally more energy than older children and adults, but they have small stomachs. In order for children to get sufficient energy they need energy-rich food. This means that their food should contain a higher proportion of fat than adults' food. It is also a time when the brain is developing rapidly and requires an adequate supply of essential fatty acids. Because of this, children, between 1 and 2 years, should be given full fat milk to drink. If they are eating well and there are no concerns about their growth they can have semi-skimmed milk from 2 years of age and skimmed milk from 5 years of age. Skimmed and semi-skimmed milk can, however, be used in food preparation from 2 years.

Young children should not be given too much fibre in their diet. Fibre is indigestible and 'bulks out' food, reducing the energy density. Fibre has also been shown to stop the absorption of some nutrients in the stomach, resulting in deficiencies if too much is consumed (British Nutrition Foundation, 2007).

Because of their small stomachs, children will need to be given healthy snacks in between meals, although this should not be to the detriment of them eating their main meal.

The government recommendations are that children of this age are given some of the following foods every day:

▸ milk and dairy products

▸ meat, fish and eggs, beans, peas and lentils. It is recommended that boys can be given up to four portions of oily fish a week, whereas girls should only be given two. Beans, peas and lentils are particularly important for those being weaned on to a vegetarian diet

▸ bread and other cereals such as pasta, potatoes and other starch vegetables

▸ fruit and vegetables.

There are some foods that young children should avoid:

▸ raw eggs and foods containing partially cooked eggs because of the risk of salmonella

▸ whole or chopped nuts because of the risk of choking

▸ shark, swordfish and marlin because of high mercury levels

▸ raw shellfish which may cause food poisoning

▸ salt should not be added to food; children of this age should be having no more than 2 g of salt a day

▸ do not add sugar or honey to children's food

▸ sweet and fizzy drinks because the sugar in them will cause tooth decay.

Many children in early childhood settings spend most of their waking hours in the nursery. It is not uncommon for children to arrive at eight in the morning and be collected at six in the evening. It is vital, therefore, that nurseries make the provision for food the highest priority. In the UK various local authorities have written their own guidance to aid early years practitioners to plan to provide good nutrition whilst children are on their premises. None of this will be possible without a whole-team approach to the development of policies and procedures that take into account the particular context of the setting.

Case study

When a new children's centre was set up in a deprived area of inner-city London, the centre head realized that many of the children would be attending from 8.30 a.m. to 4.50 p.m. for 48 weeks a year. She knew that, for most of the children, the meals they ate at nursery were their main source of food. Knowing what she did about the importance of optimum nutrition not only for physical health but also for learning, she decided to make the provision of high-quality meals a priority. These are some of the measures she took.

▸ At the planning stage she discussed the provision of a kitchen where meals could be prepared on site.

▸ She withdrew the nursery from the borough-wide school-meals service, provided by a central contractor, and retained full control of meal provision.

▸ She allocated extra resources for buying high-quality ingredients.

▸ The staff team were all involved in producing a centre policy about food provision so that everyone understood what was trying to be achieved.

▸ A community dietician was involved from the start of the venture. The dietician worked with the centre's cook to plan appropriate menus that met the nutritional and individual needs of the children. Food was to be as fresh as possible and as free from additives as possible.

▸ The food was bought directly by the centre from suppliers. One of the big supermarkets became involved and negotiated good rates for organic fruit, vegetables, fish and meat. Over 60 per cent of the food given to the children was organic.

(Continued)

▸ The kitchen became the hub of the nursery with meal-times being key times within the nursery day.

▸ The garden was used to grow fresh produce on site, with parents and children helping.

Investigate the following documents, and any document that your local authority may have produced and discuss them with your colleagues. On the basis of what you find out, review the food and drink provision in your setting.

www.scotland.gov.uk/Publications/2006/01/18153659/0 This is the link to the Scottish Execurive document 'Nutritional guidance for early years: food choices for children 1–5 in early education and childcare settings'.

www.dfes.gov.uk/schoollunches/downloads/H01530Nursery.pdf This is the link to the DfES guidance for those providing meals in nursery schools and classes.

Providing food and drink for children 5–8 years (school guidelines)

From the age of 5, children can follow the guidelines for healthy eating for adults. They are growing fast, so they have proportionately higher energy needs than adults so healthy snacks are appropriate. When providing food for this age child it is important to remember to include the following foods:

▸ foods rich in calcium such as milk, cheese, yoghurt, soya beans, tofu and nuts

▸ foods rich in vitamin D such as fortified cereals, margarine and oily fish

▸ foods rich in iron such as red meat, liver, pulses, green vegetables and fortified breakfast cereal

▸ two portions of fish a week, to provide protein, unsaturated oils and vitamins. Fish is a good source of omega 3 fatty acids

▸ foods rich in vitamin C such as citrus fruit, tomatoes and potatoes

▸ foods rich in vitamin A such as milk, margarine, butter, green vegetables, carrots and apricots

▸ drinks should be restricted to water and milk with fruit juices and squash being limited to meal-times.

Foods to limit include salt; 5-year-olds should have a maximum of 3 g a day, whilst 7-year-olds should have no more than 5 g daily. Sticky, sweet foods eaten between meals not only increase the risk of obesity, but promote dental disease, so the consumption of sweets, biscuits, sweetened drinks and cakes should be limited, preferably to once a week after a meal. Children should be encouraged to clean their teeth afterwards. Salty, fatty snacks, such as crisps, should also be eaten only occasionally (FSA, 2007b).

In May 2006 the government announced new standards for school lunches, as a response to growing professional and public unease about the quality of food provided to children in school. The standards will eventually cover all food and drink provided in schools and is being gradually phased in. Under the interim standards (School Food Trust 2007) the following foods should be on the school lunch menu:

- at least two servings of fruit and vegetables, with one being vegetable or salad and one being fruit

- two portions of fish a week, one of which should be an oily fish, to provide unsaturated oils and vitamins. Oily fish are a good source of omega 3

- a type of bread with no fat or oil should be provided every day

- free, fresh drinking water should be provided

- drinks provided should be still or sparkling water, skimmed or semi-skimmed milk, fruit and vegetable juices, plain soya, rice or oat drinks enriched with calcium, and plain yogurt drinks. Tea, coffee and low-calorie chocolate are also permitted.

Foods that are not permitted or are restricted:

- confectionery (biscuits and sweets)

- salt must not be provided

- condiments such as mayonnaise or ketchup should only be supplied in individual sachets

- snacks such as crisps must not be provided. Healthy snacks, such as nuts, seeds, vegetables and fruit are permitted as long as there is no added fat, salt or sugar. Breadsticks and savoury crackers can be served as long as they are part of a meal containing vegetables, fruit or dairy products

- deep fried products such as chips are restricted to twice a week

- meat products from each of the following four groups can only be served once a fortnight:

- burgers, chopped meat and corned beef

- sausages and sausage meat

- meat pies/sausage rolls

- any other shaped or coated meat product (School Food Trust, 2007).

Summary

▸ There is overwhelming evidence that what we eat can influence our state of health. In the UK the Scientific Advisory Committee takes an evidence-based approach and advises the government on what advice should be given to the population on healthy eating.

▸ There is specific dietary advice for women before, during and after pregnancy.

▸ Babies should be exclusively breastfed until the age of 6 months, when they should be gradually weaned on to solid food.

▸ There are specific dietary guidelines for children from 1 to 5, who have smaller stomachs than older children and need small frequent, energy-rich meals.

▸ Children over 5 can be given meals that conform to the adult guidelines.

▸ Nutritional standards are being introduced for the provision of meals in schools.

Discussion points

▸ In the UK there are very few mothers who exclusively breastfeed until a child is 6 months and the majority of babies appear fit and well despite being introduced to other foods by 4 months of age. How appropriate is it to continue to recommend the WHO guidelines?

▸ Do the present courses in childcare and education adequately equip practitioners to develop appropriate nutrition policies and procedures within early years settings?

Further reading

Caroline Walker Trust (expert working party) (2006) *Eating well for Under Fives in Childcare: Practical and Nutritional Guidelines* (2nd ed), St Austell: Caroline Walker Trust.

Useful web sites

www.nutrition.org.uk/The web site of the British Nutrition Foundation. www.eatwell.gov.uk/ Healthy eating section from the Food Standards Agency. www.schoolfoodtrust.org.uk/ The web site for the School Food Trust.

www.scotland.gov.uk/Publications/2006/01/18153659/0 This is the link to the Scottish Executive document 'Nutritional guidance for early years: food choices for children 1–5 in early education and childcare settings'

(All accessed 25 July 2007.)

Health Inequalities

In this chapter, we look at how the health and well-being of individuals is influenced by socio-economic factors, with particular reference to nutritional status. We investigate which parts of the world are most likely to experience food poverty and how globalization affects nutrition in countries in transition. We explore how health inequalities persist in the minority world and how factors such as geography, class, race, gender and disability can all have an impact on health and nutritional status.

In Chapter 2 we noted that 30 per cent of children born into the world today will suffer from malnutrition. Sadly we are familiar with media images of children from the majority world suffering from lack of food. There are many millions of families who do not have sufficient resources to meet even the most basic of their needs; these families are living in **absolute poverty**. In the UK the state benefit system ensures that almost no one lives in absolute poverty and yet there are still differences in the nutritional status of children in families living in **relative poverty** (Townsend, 1979). Economic status has, perhaps, the most pervasive influence on children's nutrition and health; however, other factors such as social class, education, race, gender and ability can all contribute to health inequalities

The following key areas are explored:

▸ Global poverty and health inequalities

▸ Countries in transition and the effect of globalization

▸ Health inequalities in Europe and the UK

▸ Health inequalities and children's nutrition

▸ Nutritional inequalities within families.

Global poverty and health inequalities

The majority of people in the world live in conditions of poverty; an often quoted statistic is that half the population live on less than US$ 2 a day (World

Bank, 2001). There are huge differences in the **gross domestic product** (GDP) per person between different countries, from US$68,800 in Luxembourg to US$600 in Malawi (CIA, 2007). There are also large inequalities within countries between the very rich and the very poor. In 2006 Denmark was calculated as being the most economically equal society, with Namibia having the largest gap between the richest and the poorest inhabitants (UN, 2006).

One of the consequences of poverty is poor health, as measured by life expectancy, childhood mortality, hunger and malnutrition, with the result that in the poorest 50 countries life expectancy at birth is 48.7 years compared with 74.8 years in the 50 richest countries (ESRC, 2006).

The World Health Organization is a multinational organization, representing 193 states, set up by the United Nations (UN) with the objective of helping people attain the highest possible level of health. In September 2000, the WHO adopted the UN Millennium Declaration, setting out goals to be reached by 2015. 'The Millennium Goals include challenges for rich and poor countries alike. They set targets for developing countries to reduce poverty and hunger, and to tackle ill-health, gender inequality, lack of education, lack of access to clean water and environmental degradation' (WHO, 2005a: 1). Three of these goals relate specifically to health:

▸ To reduce child mortality.

▸ To improve maternal health.

▸ To combat diseases such as HIV and malaria.

Every year the WHO publishes a global report. In 2005 the report focused on child, infant and maternal health and commented upon the progress made towards the achievement of the Millennium Goals. The report noted that even now,

> Each year 3.3 million babies – or maybe even more – are stillborn, more than 4 million die within 28 days of coming into the world, and a further 6.6 million young children die before their fifth birthday. Maternal deaths also continue unabated – the annual total now stands at 529 000 often sudden, unpredicted deaths which occur during pregnancy itself (some 68 000 as a consequence of unsafe abortion), during childbirth, or after the baby has been born. (WHO, 2005b)

The report noted that although some progress had been made, the countries with the worst health records were making the least progress, with the situation actually worsening in some countries. Health inequalities between poor and rich countries and between the poor and rich within countries have continued to increase. The reasons for a worsening situation in some countries were put down to:

- persistent poverty

- lack of money to invest in child and maternal health programmes

- difficulties in managing programmes effectively

- humanitarian crises resulting from war, natural disasters and climate change

- HIV epidemics

- all of the above contributing to economic downturn and a health workforce crisis.

Activity

www.povertymap.net/mapsgraphics/graphics/Undernutrition_en.jpg (accessed 28 July 2007).

This gives a good overview of the parts of the world where children are suffering the effects of under-nutrition.

In Chapter 2 we looked in some detail at the effects of under-nutrition on children. Poor nutrition not only has consequences for individual children, but has consequences for the countries they live in:

- The increased levels of infant and childhood mortality due to malnutrition means that there will be fewer economically active adults in the future.

- Malnourished children are less able to contribute to the economy in the future owing to poor health, time off school (even if schooling is available) and learning difficulties due to lack of nutrition.

There is a complex relationship between malnutrition and HIV/Aids. In some parts of the world, there are no longer sufficient people to farm the land, and there are large numbers of orphan children being cared for by grandparents. This has led to malnutrition in the surviving population, who are then more susceptible to infections and the effects of HIV/Aids (Oxfam, 2002).

Poor countries find themselves in the grip of a vicious cycle where poverty fuels malnutrition, which has a negative effect on the economic viability of the community, resulting in increased levels of poverty.

Activity

There is much debate about the role richer countries have played in the cause and perpetuation of global poverty. It is important that we all are aware of the wider issues and the part that we may be able to play as individuals. The following web sites will give you information.

UNICEF UK, www.unicef.org.uk/aboutus/index.asp

Make Poverty History, www.makepovertyhistory.org/

Globalization and Global Poverty Challenge, www.globalpovertychallenge.com/

Global Poverty Research Group, www.gprg.org/

Global Call to Action Against Poverty, www.whiteband.org/

(All accessed on 28 July 2007.)

Countries in transition and the effect of globalization

In the UK, since the middle of the twentieth century, there has been a remarkable change in the way that we shop, cook and eat. We have made a transition from:

- fresh food brought daily, to the increasing use of chilled/frozen foods and foods with a long shelf life
- meals produced from basic ingredients, to pre-prepared products (often high in fats, sugars and additives)
- food produced locally, to food being imported from all over the world
- foods being eaten in season, to foods being available all the year round
- small producers, to large, international, industrial-sized producers
- meals being eaten in the home, to meals being eaten outside
- foods being chosen for taste, freshness, and so on, to foods being chosen by brand name and lifestyle image.

There are real concerns about the environmental impact of transporting food all over the world and the danger of eating pre-prepared foods that are high in fats, sugar and additives, but many of us welcome the choice that is available in our supermarkets. The impact on small shops in the high street may worry us, but the convenience of being able to shop once a week, or online, is valued by many. We may feel uneasy about the impact of advertising on the food choices made by and for children but, for many people, a trip to a popular fast-food outlet is a normal part of life (Martens and Warde, 1997).

These changes have been fuelled, in part, by the process of **globalization**, resulting in many of the foods and food products that we have become familiar with being available throughout the world. The process of globalization is not just a phenomenon of richer countries such as the UK, the USA and Japan; the process can be seen in poorer countries as well. These countries, like the UK before them, are undergoing a process of **nutrition transition**. In the majority world, despite many of the population being malnourished, the consumption of foods high in fats and sugars is increasing amongst those who can afford it. There is a corresponding decrease in the amount of cereals in the diet and a decrease in the amount of fruit and vegetables consumed. This **obesogenic** diet has caused an epidemic of obesity-related diseases worldwide. Although we consider obesity and all the health-related conditions that go with it to be a problem for the richer countries of the minority world, there are now more people dying of heart disease in poorer countries of the majority world. Within different countries there are great health inequalities, with the problem being more serious among the poor (Hawks, 2006). In addition, the obesogenic diet is associated with micronutrient deficiencies that lower immunity to infectious diseases, which has a much greater impact on the health of populations in poorer countries than wealthier ones.

Case study: Kolkata, a city in transition

Penny started visiting Kolkata (formerly known as Calcutta) in West Bengal, India, over 30 years ago. At that time, Kolkata, once the capital of British India, was a bustling, chaotic and noisy city. Being near the border with Bangladesh, Kolkata had absorbed wave after wave of refugees, as well as receiving many thousands of rural Indians from the hinterlands, all hoping to make a living in the city. There was dire poverty, with thousands who only had the pavement as their home, and millions living in slum areas. Even for the emerging middle classes, life was not easy, with food shortages and power cuts being a regular feature of life.

There were no supermarkets, fresh produce being purchased daily as few households had the luxury of a refrigerator. Most people ate only in their own homes, with a diet consisting mainly of rice, lentils and

(Continued)

(Continued)

vegetables. Those who could afford it would try to have fish most days, but meat was for special occasions; many families were vegetarian. Outside the home only the very wealthy could afford to eat in a restaurant, with office workers eating simple snacks prepared by wayside venders if they could afford it. Thirty years on, the situation has radically changed. Although there is still a distressingly high 70 per cent rate of malnutrition among the children of pavement and slum dwellers (Ray et al., 1999), amongst better-off families the rate of obesity is rising. In 2005 it was estimated that between 30 and 40 per cent of children in the 3 to 11 age group in Kolkata were obese (Majumdar, 2005). One contributing factor is a change in food habits. Hundreds of fast-food outlets have sprung up around the city, selling 'Western style' burgers and pizzas to an increasingly affluent middle class. Ice cream and fizzy drinks are available on every street corner and the shops are full of pre-prepared meals, crisps, biscuits and sugary drinks. Within the home, increasing affluence has meant that foods normally reserved for 'treats' are eaten more often and many more children can afford the tempting snacks that are sold in the street. As in the UK, advertisements on the television are targeted at children, to the extent that children are influencing the choice of foods purchased from the increasing number of supermarkets that have been built.

Recently, the more educated sector of the population is becoming aware of the health effects of the obesogenic lifestyle and individuals are choosing to eat healthily and to exercise. Concern is being expressed in the media about the numbers of adults suffering from diabetes and heart disease, but the message has yet to filter down to the majority of the population.

▶ What are the advantages and disadvantages of the opening up of Kolkata to global influences?

▶ In what way was a typical diet of 30 years ago healthier than now?

▶ What strategies could be employed to reduce the level of childhood obesity?

▶ What about the street children and the children of the slum dwellers; what initiatives could be taken to help them?

Health inequalities in Europe and the UK

There have been dramatic changes in the health of people living in Europe over the past 150 years. One measure of health is life expectancy. In 1851, life expectancy at birth in England and Wales was 40 years for males and 44 years for females (Newton, 2006). Now, babies born in England in 2004 can expect to live until they are 76 if they are male and 80 if they are female. There are a variety of reasons behind this dramatic improvement in health in the UK:

▸ The huge investment in public health started by the Victorians means that we now have clean water to drink, effective sewerage and rubbish disposal.

▸ Investment in housing, with inner-city slum areas being regenerated.

▸ Medical advances including prevention of disease by vaccination and the treatment of infectious diseases by antibiotics.

▸ The reduction of absolute poverty by the introduction of Social Security benefits for those in need.

▸ The advent of the National Health Service in 1948.

Health inequalities in the UK

However, although the general health of the nation was improving, some sectors of the population were doing less well than others. In 1980 the Conservative government asked Douglas Black to investigate the difference in health between social classes in Britain. The result of the investigation was disappointing. In the Foreword to the report (Black et al., 1980) Patrick Jenkin, the Secretary for State for Social Services, said:

> It will come as a disappointment to many that over long periods since the inception of the NHS there is generally little sign of health inequalities in Britain actually diminishing and in some cases, they may be increasing. It will be seen that the Group has reached the view that the causes of health inequalities are so deep rooted that only a major and wide-ranging programme of public expenditure is capable of altering the pattern.

The report noted that social class differences in health, as measured by mortality, started at birth. In 1971, deaths within the first month of life were twice as high for children born of fathers in the lowest social class than for children born of fathers in the highest social class. This differential remained throughout life, so that the death rate for adult males from the lowest social class was twice as high as those from the highest social class.

The Black report was published over a bank holiday weekend and it was widely thought that the Conservative government wanted to suppress the findings because of ideological and resource implications.

In 1997, the newly elected Labour government asked Sir Donald Acheson to update the report. His findings, based on statistics for England and Wales, were similar to those of Douglas Black and his team:

▸ Average mortality has fallen over the last 50 years.

▸ Health inequalities have remained the same or, for some sectors of society, have increased (Acheson, 1998).

Acheson found significant inequalities:

▸ across classes, with people in the lower socio-economic groups having poorer health than those in the highest groups

▸ between different racial, cultural and religious groups, with black and South Asian groups having more ill health than the white population, whereas people of Chinese origin appear to have better health than the white population

▸ between the sexes, with women having better health than men

▸ across the age range, with younger people having better health than the elderly.

Why do these inequalities persist, given the improvements in public health and medical interventions? Black et al. (1980) outline four possible explanations:

▸ *Artefact explanations.* Both 'health' and 'social class' are artificial categories constructed to reflect social organization and are so difficult to define that any 'measurment' is fraught with difficulties and may not represent an underlying 'truth'. The way that social class is categorized has changed over the years.

▸ *Natural and social selection.* This explanation derives from the idea that individuals are in the lowest social class because they have worse ill health than others. Those individuals who have good health will obtain education and occupations higher up the social classification. So one would expect the strongest and fittest individuals to be in the higher social classes. In other words, illness itself is a factor in confining an individual to the lower social class.

▸ *Poverty leads to ill health*, through nutrition, housing and environment. Thus, people in the lowest social class have fewer material resources, which has a direct effect on health.

▸ *Cultural and behavioural explanations.* In this explanation the people in the lowest social class are responsible for their own ill health because of poor health behaviours. The reason, for instance, that levels of obesity are highest in the lowest social class, is that they have not changed to a healthy diet.

A close examination of these explanations will show that none fully accounts for the health inequalities seen in society today.

As a result of the Acheson report the government made tackling health inequalities a priority and in 2002 a **cross-cutting review** was published outlining progress made. At that time it was confirmed that wide-ranging inequalities were still exerting a powerful influence on the nation's health (Hyder and Mukherji, 2004).

In July 2003 the government launched 'Tackling Health Inequalities, a Programme for Action'. The main aim of the programme is to reduce inequalities in health outcomes by 10 per cent as measured by infant mortality and life expectancy at birth by 2010. These aims were designated as **public service agreement** targets (PSAs). The Health Inequalities Unit was set up to oversee the cross-governmental programme. One of the aims is to support families, mothers and children. Key initiatives under this aim are the Sure Start initiative and the introduction of Child Tax Credit. This approach to tackling health inequalities is common across the whole of the UK, with similar initiatives being taken in Scotland, Northern Ireland and Wales.

Within each country in the UK, there is a commitment to regular monitoring of the progress of the various health initiatives. In October 2006 the *Health Profile of England* (DoH, 2006b) was published, which provided a picture of the health of people living in England in 2004. The findings showed that, although there was an overall improvement in determinants of health in some areas such as the reduction of smoking, improved housing stock and a reduction in child poverty, there were still areas of concern, such as levels of obesity and high levels of teenage pregnancy. Health inequalities were still pervasive and, although the gap between disadvantaged areas and the national average for cancer and circulatory disease had improved, the figures relating to the two targets had increased:

▸ Infant **mortality rates** had declined in lower socio-economic groups, but the rate of decline was faster in other groups, so the gap continued to widen.

▸ The relative gap in life expectancy between areas in England with the worst health deprivation and figures for England as a whole had widened (DoH, 2006a).

Health inequalities within European countries

Within individual European countries health inequalities, as described for the UK, exist. Bartley (2004) investigated the extent of health inequalities in several European countries. She explains how differences in the way that health and social stratification are measured between different countries makes comparisons difficult, but she concluded that, as in the UK, health inequalities were increasing in all the countries she investigated. In Nordic countries the rise in health difference between different social economic groups was less than in other European countries.

When the UK took over the European Union (EU) presidency in 2005, health inequalities across Europe became a key health theme and reports to look at health challenges facing Europe were commissioned. In one report, Mackenbach (2006) confirms that widespread health inequalities within the different countries of the EU continue to exist. In tandem with this report, a paper by Judd et al. (2006) explored the different approaches made by various EU countries to tackle the problem. The main conclusions are that, although attempts were being made to focus initiatives towards the most disadvantaged sections of communities, the underlying cause of health inequality, the social gradient, was not being tackled directly by any country.

Health inequalities and children's nutrition

In 1999, the British Medical Association (BMA) stressed that one of the most important factors in children's nutritional status is adequate income and it is now universally accepted that the nutritional status of children is one aspect of health that is directly linked to **indices of poverty and disadvantage**. Indeed the adverse effects of poor nutrition in childhood may be the main reason that we see health inequalities persist from one generation to another (Nelson, 2000). But how do poverty and disadvantage affect the nutritional status of children living in the UK?

▸ The 2005 Infant Feeding Survey continues to show, as it has done since it was first initiated, that the numbers of mothers breastfeeding their children is related to indices of disadvantage, such as social class and level of education (Information Centre for Health and Social Care, 2007).

▸ Children living in poverty often have diets that lack fruit and vegetables, and contain levels of fat and sugar that are too high. Graham and Power (2004) link this to negative effects on children's ability to learn, and a risk of infection and cardiovascular disease in adulthood. Poverty can also lead to children being overweight or underweight for their height. The National Children's Homes (NCH) undertook a study of 55 families on a low income and found that 28 per cent never ate green vegetables or salad and 10 per cent of children never ate fruit. The study concluded that it cost more to eat healthily than unhealthily (NCH, 2004).

▸ Children from impoverished families are more likely to have diets lacking in the nutrients required to maintain an effective immune system and are more prone to infections (Nelson, 2000).

▶ There are well documented links between poverty, disadvantage and dental disease. Young children living in the poorest, non-fluoridated communities were six times more likely to suffer from dental disease than children from more advantaged, fluoridated communities (National Alliance for Equity in Dental Health (NAEDH), 2000).

Reducing nutritional inequalities

There are three main approaches to reducing nutritional inequalities in children:

▶ measures aimed at reducing child poverty

▶ measures aimed at improving access and availability of healthy food in disadvantaged areas

▶ measures aimed at supporting individuals in making healthy choices.

Reducing child poverty

The government has made a commitment to reduce child poverty in the UK and has set itself the target of eradicating child poverty by 2020, with a reduction of a quarter by 2005. In March 2006, the Department of Work and Pensions published figures that indicated that the 2005 target had been narrowly missed, with a 23 per cent reduction; however, 5.8 million children are still defined as living in poverty (DWP, 2006). That we still have a long way to go in reducing child poverty has been recognized in the government document *Working for Children* (DWP, 2007), which outlines a variety of initiatives aimed at helping parents into work, with the expectation that this will increase income in vulnerable families.

Activity

Investigate the Child Poverty Action Group web site, www.cpag.org.uk/

What proportion of children that you care for could be classified as living in poverty? Do you think that it is part of your professional role to support organisations such as this?

Investigate the document *Working for Children*. Make a list of the initiatives set in place with the aim of reducing child poverty.

www.dwp.gov.uk/publications/dwp/2007/childpoverty/childpoverty.pdf

(Both web sites accessed 28 July 2007.)

Improving access and availability of healthy foods

One of the difficulties facing families in poverty is that sometimes it is difficult for them to access healthy foods. This inability to find healthy and affordable food is sometimes known as **Food poverty**. According to Tim Lang (Sustain, 2007) 'Food poverty is worse diet, worse access, worse health, higher percentage of income on food and less choice from a restricted range of foods. Above all food poverty is about less or almost no consumption of fruit & vegetables'.

There are a variety of factors that can lead to food poverty including:

▸ *lack of shops in the area*. Some areas of social housing are out of town and it is difficult for those on a low income to afford the cost of transport to shops or supermarkets

▸ *limited range of healthy food in local shops*. Some areas of the UK have been described as 'food deserts' where it is impossible to buy healthy food at affordable prices

▸ *lack of income* can lead to parents having to buy cheaper, less nutritious food

▸ *Fear of crime* can deter individuals from travelling to shops where healthy food is available.

Tackling food poverty requires co-ordinated action between central and local government working in conjunction with local community organizations, and includes initiatives such as:

▸ The UK Healthy Start Scheme, outlined in Chapter 1. This is designed to improve nutrition for pregnant women, mothers and young children by making healthy foods such as fruit and vegetables more easily available.

▸ The Sure Start initiative that was designed to give children in deprived areas the best start in life.

▸ The Free School Meal Scheme.

Chapter 8 looks in more detail at multidisciplinary approaches to improving children's diets.

Supporting individuals in making healthy choices

There is a persistent view that dietary health inequalities in lower socio-economic groups are perpetuated because of lack of knowledge about what constitutes a healthy diet, or a lack of will to implement this knowledge. This belief that individual attitudes and behaviours are amenable to change under-pins a variety of health promotion initiatives, some of which are investigated in Chapter 7. Thus, the onus for tackling dietary health inequalities is seen to rest with the individual, and where the health of children is concerned the focus is primarily on the parents. However, there is a wealth of evidence (Atree, 2006) that suggests that most mothers are well aware of what constitutes a healthy diet for their children, but are constrained by lack of money and all the other factors mentioned previously that contribute to food poverty. One woman summed up the dilemma of how to feed her family on a reduced budget as follows:

> We try to eat proper meals like meat and veg. and that but there just isn't the money to do it all the time. So we eat properly maybe once or twice a week depending on the money and the rest of the time we make do with things like sausages, pies, potatoes and things like beans. The meals aren't as good but they do the job, they'll fill them (children) up and stop them from being hungry. It's the best I can do. (Atree, 2006: 72)

It is unlikely that health promotion campaigns on their own will have much of an effect on the nutritional status of children from disadvantaged families unless there is a co-ordinated approach that aims to alleviate poverty and increase access to healthy food.

Reflection point

In Chapter 7 you will be looking at how to promote healthy eating in early years settings. How could you use the research findings on the effects of health promotion on lower-income groups to help plan your initiative?

Nutritional inequalities within families

So far, this chapter has looked primarily at the impact of social class and poverty on nutrition and people's health. We need to be careful, when thinking about inequality, that we do not assume that individuals *within* a family have the same access to a nutritious diet. Women, in particular, have a different experience of food and eating within families, on the whole, than men.

Fischler's (1988) work in relation to food and eating notes that within some families there are different entitlements to the types and quantities of food men and women eat. DeVault's (1997) work demonstrates that there is an expectation that men will receive 'man-sized' portions of food and 'decent food', often viewed as food that a woman has taken trouble to prepare. Fitchen's (1997) American study showed that, when feeding a family is difficult owing to poverty, some individuals within the family go underfed. Whilst she did not gather any quantitative data around this, her observations show that children often have a different experience of going hungry than adult males. An example might be through denial of some foods and smaller sized portions, with children with disabilities or who are vulnerable in other ways – such as being children from a previous marriage – being disproportionately affected. Women, in particular, take less of the meat and vegetables they give to the rest of their family and in very poor households, were found to live primarily on starchy foods such as pasta, tortillas and potatoes. This impacts negatively on their health in terms of obesity, poor dental health and, generally, a low nutritional status, factors noted by professionals who work with low-income women in the USA. If pregnant or breastfeeding their children, this might also have a negative impact on the health of the child.

Many people in Fitchen's (1997) study had experienced poverty and hunger as children and suffered food anxiety as adults. Fitchen suggests that this anxiety carries over to subsequent generations. In low-income families, her study found that food was the source of considerable tension, with many family arguments centred round the lack of food or having to make do with food of poorer quality. Ellis (1983) argues that domestic violence incidents, for instance, are often triggered by men complaining about how food is prepared and served in the home. This is not necessarily linked to income. Given that domestic violence often begins during pregnancy and impacts in a range of ways that adversely affect children's emotional health (Humphreys, 2001), we need to take very seriously the way power is exercised around food within families.

Reflection point

Reflect upon your own experience of meal-times. In your experience, do men have differing amounts of certain foods when compared with women? An example might be giving an adult male a greater quantity of meat or the best cut of meat when compared with women.

Summary

▸ There are great inequalities in wealth across the world with the majority of the world's population living in poverty.

▸ Under-nutrition is both an effect and a cause of poverty.

▸ Increasing globalization has led to a change in dietary habits in both the minority and the majority world, resulting in a global rise in childhood obesity.

▸ Despite the eradication of absolute poverty in the UK and Europe there are still deep and pervasive inequalities in health across socio-economic groups.

▸ There has been a reduction in child poverty in the UK yet there are still profound differences in the nutritional status of children across socio-economic groups. These nutritional inequalities are, perhaps, the reason for persistent health inequalities across the age range.

▸ It is important to remember that inequalities exist within families. Access to food may be differently experienced by men, women and children.

Discussion points

▸ Do early years settings have a moral responsibility to consider global ethical issues such as the promotion of 'Fair Trade' and using locally sourced produce when planning for the children's nutrition?

▸ To what extent should your setting become involved in local community initiatives to increase food accessibility?

Further reading

Atree, P. (2006) 'A critical analysis of UK public health policies in relation to diet and nutrition in low income families', *Maternal and Child Nutrition*, 2: 67–78.

Graham, H. (2007) *Unequal Lives: Health and Socio-Economic Inequalities.* Maidenhead: Open University Press.

Nelson, M. (2000) 'Childhood nutrition and poverty', *Proceedings of the Nutrition Society*, 59: 307–15.

Useful web sites

www.sochealth.co.uk/history/black.htm This web site gives the whole of the Black report with some interesting commentaries that give the historical context.

www.archive.official-documents.co.uk/document/doh/ih/ih.htm This site gives the whole of the Acheson report.

(Both accessed 28 July 2007.)

Food, Eating and Emotion

The eating behaviour of children (and adults) is influenced by a complex set of interacting factors. This chapter looks at the physiological processes and psychological underpinnings of hunger and how early childhood experiences, especially early attachment relationships, may have an effect on subsequent eating behaviour. Infant feeding and eating difficulties are discussed, together with the role of early years practitioners in promoting positive experiences for children regarding food and meal-times.

This chapter looks at food and eating from an individual perspective and begins with a look at some of the underlying physiological processes that influence eating behaviour. We will emphasize that purely physiological explanations do not explain why it is that we eat when we are not hungry and we explore some psychological explanations, including psychoanalytic explanations, that look at underlying attachment processes.

The following key areas are explored.

- The physiological processes underlying eating behaviour
- Impulsivity and eating behaviour
- Stress, depression and eating
- The influence of early feeding experiences
- Feeding and eating disorders
- Promoting positive attitudes towards food in early years settings.

The physiological processes underlying eating behaviour

Homeostasis

Hunger and thirst are considered to be **physiological drives**, and are related to the concept of **homeostasis.** According to Cardwell et al. (1998) the term 'homeostasis' was first used by Cannon in 1932, to describe the mechanism by which our bodies try to keep internal processes in balance. The body works best when there is a correct balance of chemicals, nutrients, oxygen and water available at the correct temperature. If, for example, the proportion of water changes just a few per cent, the brain would not function and a change in body temperature of more than a few degrees would result in death. Homeostasis is the process of keeping bodily mechanisms in balance and much of our behaviour is directed at homeostatic control (Mukherji, 2001). If we have not eaten for a while, our bodies become short of energy and physiological processes will be set in motion that initiate within us a drive to eat (hunger). Once we have eaten the drive to eat is reduced.

Of course, it is not quite this simple. When we eat it takes time before the food is digested and the nutrients are available to be used by the body, but we finish eating before digestion is completed, so there must be other mechanisms in place that tell us when we are 'full'. In addition, in the minority world, we tend to eat regular meals so that we rarely experience intense hunger. There are obviously other factors involved.

Reflection point

Think about your own body:

▸ Are you regularly very hungry or thirsty, or does your pattern of mealtimes mean that you rarely experience strong pangs of hunger?

▸ When you eat, how do you know when to stop eating? Do you ever disregard feelings of being full by having a dessert when you do not really need one? (The common phenomenon of being too full for more dinner, but not too full for pudding!)

▸ Are there particular foods that you eat more of because you like them and other foods that you are less likely to overeat?

▸ Do you turn to certain foods for comfort?

If the only factors that influence our eating behaviour were physiological, how can we explain some of our eating behaviours?

If homeostatic mechanisms were the only influences on behaviour then, given a selection of foods that would supply all our nutritional needs, we should only eat when we needed to and should remain in perfect energy balance (correct weight for height and such like.) One experiment conducted in the 1920s seemed to suggest that this might be the case. Davis observed 15 infants from the time they were newly weaned to the age of about 4½. They were all being looked after in a residential setting and the carers were instructed to make available to them a variety of foods and let the children choose what and when to eat. The results suggested that the children thrived, and automatically chose a balanced diet. However, it should be noted that the foods made available to the children did not include foods rich in fat and sugar, and certainly no crisps and ice cream (Strauss, 2006). Our recent experience of both adults and children being at increasing risk of obesity seems to suggest that we are not very good at automatically choosing a healthy diet or maintaining correct body weight. Factors other than physiological processes are at work.

Physiological mechanisms that help control food intake

There are several mechanisms that are set in action when we eat that contribute to regulating our food intake. These are reported by Cardwell et al. (1998) as being:

▸ *The presence of food in the mouth.* People who are tube fed directly into the stomach are able to regulate body weight, which indicates that the sensation of having food in the mouth is not needed to regulate meal size, but individuals do report that the whole experience was not as satisfying, as they needed to taste and chew their food.

▸ *The presence of food in the stomach.* There appears to be a mechanism by which signals are sent from the stomach to the brain, signalling satiety (feeling full) when a normal-sized meal is eaten. The signals are sensitive to the quality of food as well as quantity as there is evidence that we feel full quicker with high-energy foods. Individuals who have the size of their stomach reduced either because of disease or to help them lose weight, do report feeling full after eating very little. However, some individuals compensate by taking small, frequent high calorie foods, and in one study 25 per cent of patients regained all the weight that they had originally lost (Sjostrom, 2004), indicating that stomach size was not the only factor in controlling food intake.

▸ *Cholecystokininin (CCK).* This is a hormone that is released from the small duodenum when it registers the presence of food. Studies have indicated that injections of CCK reduce the size of meals consumed by humans and rats (Cardwell et al., 1998). The use of CCK as an appetite suppressant is being investigated but according to Horowitz et al. (2005), it is unlikely that it will prove to be helpful in treating obesity.

Another physiological process that has an effect on appetite is the level of blood glucose in our system. We need sufficient glucose in our bloodstream because it is this that is broken down to give us energy. If our blood glucose level is low, we may feel faint and weak, and will automatically look for food. People who are diabetic and take insulin have to be particularly careful to balance the insulin with sufficient food, as they are at risk of suddenly having a dangerously low level of blood glucose and falling unconscious. The level of blood glucose is measured by gluco receptors in the blood vessels, liver and the brain, particularly the **hypothalamus**. In most individuals, however, the levels of blood glucose do not vary much as the body will convert fat stores into glucose. So glucose levels are not thought to have a significant effect on appetite levels (Cardwell et al., 1998).

The role of the hypothalamus

The hypothalamus also has an important part to play in the regulation of eating behaviour. The hypothalamus is a structure at the base of the brain (about the size of a thumb). Together with the pituitary gland it helps to control many bodily processes by regulating the formation and release of hormones (chemical messengers). There are two main centres in the hypothalamus that are implicated in eating behaviour, the ventro medial nucleus (VMN) and the lateral nucleus (LN)

▸ Research in the late 1940s showed that lesions to the VMN in rats resulted in the rats overeating to such an extent that they became massively overweight (Eysenck, 2004).

▸ In the early 1950s it was shown that lesions in the LN inhibited eating behaviour in rats so that they lost weight (Eysenck, 2004).

Eysenck (2004) considers that subsequent research supports the idea that the hypothalamus has an important role in eating behaviour, and that other areas in the brain concerned with emotional responses, such as the frontal cortex and the amygdala, are also involved. However, reviewing the evidence, he concludes that the theory exaggerates the role of the brain in controlling hunger.

Impulsivity and eating behaviour

Research indicates that obese individuals tend to show more of a preference for high-fat, energy-rich foods than those of normal weight (Skinner et al., 2004) and to eat more of these foods than people with no weight problem (Stubbs and Lee, 2004). One of the reasons may be that eating behaviour is triggered by the taste and smell of food, and that these triggers have a more powerful effect on obese individuals. Nederkoorn et al. (2006) suggest that this is due to a deficit in impulse control. In a study of obese children, it was found that these children had less inhibitory control than that of a control group of children of normal weight, and that obese children who had episodes of bingeing were more impulsive than obese children who did not binge. A lack of impulse control has global effects, not just on eating behaviour. There was a higher than usual rate of attention deficit hyperactivity disorder (ADHD) in obese children compared with children of normal weight in this study.

There are three possible explanations for the link between obesity and ADHD:

1 One of the symptoms of ADHD is lack of impulse control, which renders the child less able to resist tasty food.

2 The poor diet of an obese child can promote ADHD in susceptible individuals.

3 The stress of the condition predisposes children to comfort eat.

The link between obesity and ADHD has been reported in adults, with the highest rates of ADHD being seen in the most overweight individuals (Altfas, 2002). This link between ADHD and obesity has led to some doctors prescribing ADHD medication to obese children. Although there seems to be a degree of success with this treatment, there are concerns because the drugs have not been authorized for this purpose (Cohen, 2007).

Stress, depression and eating

There is a strong relationship between stress and eating. Most of us, at some time or other, have turned to a favourite food when stressed; usually foods such as chocolate or other high-fat, high-carbohydrate foods.

Reflection point

▸ Is there a connection between stress and eating in your life?

▸ What foods do you characteristically turn to?

▸ What sort of emotions/feelings/thoughts do you have before, during and after consuming food in these situations?

What is the connection between stress and eating? It has long been noted that there is an association between depression and obesity (Laitinen et al., 2002) Depression seems to affect people's eating habits in two different ways. In some people depression is associated with high levels of anxiety, sleeplessness, lack of appetite and weight loss. For others, depression is characterized by increased appetite, excessive sleep and weight gain (Marano, 2006).

Marano suggests that eating, as a response to stress, is related to the physiological mechanisms in the body that help us deal with situations of perceived threat. In situations of acute threat, for example if you think you are in danger of being attacked, there is an immediate physiological response by the body. This response, which is not under our conscious control, prepares us for 'flight or fight'. The hormone cortisol is produced which activates other physiological processes to increase the amount of oxygen to the brain and prepare the body for immediate action. At times of acute stress we breathe more rapidly to increase oxygen levels and the heart beats faster to get oxygen into the brain as quickly as possible. At the same time energy, in the form of glucose, is mobilized from stores in the body ready to be used as fuel for muscles. When the immediate danger has passed the level of cortisol is reduced.

In chronic stress situations, however, the production of cortisol is not reduced. As the body perceives itself to be under constant threat there is a constant demand for fuel. In these situations it appears that the brain sends out signals that motivate us to eat high-density, energy-rich foods, such as chocolate. The energy from this food is stored as abdominal fat as this is close to the liver, where many of the energy metabolism processes occur (Marano, 2006). The deposition of abdominal fat sends messages to the brain to cut off the stress response, as reserves have been built up. There is, therefore a direct connection between eating 'comfort foods' and the reduction of stress. The connection between stress reduction and eating energy-rich foods is a powerful **reinforcer**, and comfort eating is likely to be continued as a learned behaviour even in the absence of physiological cues from the body.

It has been suggested that not only do physiological stress mechanisms result in an increase in consumption of energy-rich foods, but also, even without increasing calorie intake, chronically stressed individuals may actually put on more weight than expected from the calories they consume. Kuo et al., (2007) tested mice in stressful situations. The mice were fed either their usual diet, or a high-fat diet or a high-sugar diet. When comparing the weight of the animals, it was found that the mice on the high-fat diet put on more weight than the other mice, even though they had consumed the same amount of calories. The extra fat was laid down in the abdominal region.

What does this mean for humans? Whilst it is always unwise to make direct comparisons between humans and mice, the findings suggest that:

▸ stress influences us to eat high-fat, high-sugar foods

▸ if we are stressed and eat these energy-rich foods we will put on more weight than expected if one just took into account calorie intake.

Reflection point

If you are trying hard to reduce your weight to become healthy it may be disheartening to learn that stress can make the process harder. However, comfort eating is not the only way to make us feel less stressed. What other ways can you think of to reduce stress levels?

We have discussed how stress and depression can lead individuals to eat more and gain weight. The converse of this is also true; obesity can lead to depression. In 2003 Mustillo et al. from Duke University studied 1,000 children aged 9–16 for an eight-year period. For boys, especially, there was a relationship between obesity and depression, in that boys who remained obese during childhood and adolescence were four times as likely to become clinically depressed as boys of normal weight. Other studies have backed up the findings that obesity is related to psychological consequences; for example, in a study of obese adolescents, Sjoberg et al. (2005) found that the adolescents' feelings of shame and social isolation were associated with being clinically obese.

The link between obesity and depression is very likely to be a complex interaction between social factors and physiology; treating obesity in children is not simple as so many interrelated factors need to be taken into account.

The influence of early feeding experiences

Early feeding experiences of children are commonly thought to have a part to play in infant feeding disorders and influence future psychological well-being. It is considered that for infants to develop appropriately they need secure attachments to the main carers in their life (Atkinson et al., 1996). Attachment was first described by Bowlby (1969) and is the term used to describe the tie between infant and caregiver; the infant's tendency to try to stay as close as possible to the caregiver, and the feelings of security once closeness is attained. An attachment is built up when caregivers are responsive and sensitive to the needs of the infant. The appropriate and timely meeting of the needs of the very young infant builds up a 'representation' of the caregiver being responsive and available in the baby's mind. A secure attachment to their main caregivers promotes healthy development in children, especially the ability to separate from their caregivers and develop a sense of being an individual. Later on in life, the quality of attachments that individuals form in infancy has an effect on their ability to form appropriate adult relationships and form attachments with their children (Atkinson et al., 1996).

Activity

www.psychology.sunysb.edu/attachment/online/inge_origins.pdf (accessed 28 July 2007)

Investigate this site. It is an essay by Inge Bretherton on the historical origins of attachment theory. It was published in 1997 in *Developmental Psychology*, 28: 759–75.

Satisfactory early feeding experiences are integral to the attachment process and future well-being of infants. Research by Ainsworth et al. in 1972 indicated that the sucking and rooting behaviours of newborns were the precursors of attachment behaviours and that if the baby is allowed to take the initiative about when to feed, attachment can be strengthened. Both mother/caregiver and child have important parts to play in the feeding experience. Satter (1992: 1) comments that 'feeding is a reciprocal process that depends on the abilities and characteristics of both the parent and the child.'

The characteristics of the infant that influence the feeding relationship include:

▸ the ability of the child to indicate that they need feeding

▸ the health and developmental profile of the child.

The characteristics of the carer include:

▸ physical and emotional health (including stress levels)

▸ responsiveness and sensitivity to the infant's needs

▸ degree of control over the feeding process.

If all goes well, the infant will instinctively cry when hungry and will automatically suck on the breast or bottle to feed. Summarizing a series of research studies, Satter (1992) describes how very young babies can regulate their own food intake and, given optimal conditions, will naturally participate in the weaning process when developmentally ready. However, to do this, infants need appropriate support from their main caregivers, who must not only provide the correct food (breast or formula) but should also be sensitive to the needs of infants, feeding them when they indicate that they are hungry. In addition to this the feeding experience has to be within a social environment that is accepting and loving. This relationship is one of attunement, with the parent/caregiver being tuned in to the needs of the infant.

Satter (1992: 2) summarizes the division of responsibility in the feeding process as follows: 'The parent is responsible for what the child is offered to eat, the child is responsible for how much.' Effective feeding experiences support attachment in infants, will help them develop the ability to separate from carers and promote **individuation.**

It is often assumed that breastfeeding will promote a stronger attachment relationship than bottle-feeding. In fact Bowlby's clinical observations did not lead him to predict which method of feeding would be more successful at promoting infant–carer attachments. He considered that the quality of the experience in terms of sensitivity and responsiveness were the important factors (Britton et al., 2006). Bowlby's view was confirmed in a longitudinal study of 174 mother–infant **dyads** which found that it was the quality of mother–infant interaction that predicted the security of attachment, rather than the method of feeding (Britton et al., 2006).

Feeding and eating disorders

Feeding difficulties

At all stages of infant feeding (breastfeeding/bottle-feeding and weaning on to non-milk foods) there can be difficulties. Often these difficulties are resolved as the mother/caregiver gets to know the particular characteristics of the baby, but sometimes professional help is needed, and in the UK, health visitors are particularly skilled in supporting parents with feeding difficulties. Very occasionally the difficulties are so severe that the family is referred to a specialist service, such as the feeding and eating disorder service at Great Ormond Street Hospital.

The Consultative Group on Early Childhood Care and Development (1989) describe how Chatoor et al. (1984) grouped the causes of feeding disorder into disorders of homeostasis and disorders of attachment.

▶ *Disorders of homeostasis.* In the first two months of life, babies' physiological processes need to get into a predictable cycle of wakefulness, sleeping, feeding and elimination. Difficulties may be encountered if the child is premature, has difficulties in sucking and/or sucking and breathing at the same time. There will be problems if the child's autonomous nervous system is very reactive and the child is hypersensitive to stimulation. Congenital abnormalities can contribute to difficulties in the child establishing efficient homeostatic regulation. Mothers/caregivers play a vital role at this stage. They need to provide a supportive environment, both physical and emotional, that will help babies regulate and deal with both internal and external stimuli. Misinterpretation of the infant's cues together with too little or too much stimulation can disrupt the feeding process.

▸ *Difficulties with the attachment process.* From about two to six months the infant's main challenge is to achieve psychological attachment. As discussed previously, this is a reciprocal process between the mother/caregiver and the infant and, as such, characteristics of both can influence the process and consequently how feeding progresses. Babies who have yet to achieve homeostatic control, are irritable or hypersensitive to changes in temperature, position or sound, can be difficult to handle because carers may interpret the babies' behaviour as rejection. Sometimes there are characteristics in the mother/caregiver that inhibit the attachment process. These include maternal depression, illness, under-nutrition and stressful/chaotic family circumstances.

If caregiver–infant relationships are severely maladaptive then the child may not follow their expected growth trajectory, commonly referred to as 'failure to thrive'. The importance of appropriate mother–infant interactions has been confirmed by a study undertaken in 1998 by Lindberg et al. They investigated two groups of mother–infant dyads; one group contained children who had a history of food refusal, the other was a control group of infants with uneventful feeding experiences. The researchers investigated how mothers and infants interacted during feeding and at play, and found that the mothers of the food refusers were less sensitive to their infants and showed more controlling behaviours than did the mothers of the infants who did not have feeding difficulties. The study also showed that the infants who experienced feeding difficulties sent out less clear messages about their needs than the control group, confirming that feeding is a two-way interaction.

What are the consequences to the baby if early feeding experiences are unsatisfactory? Satter (1992) considers that insensitive feeding, which puts the emphasis on getting food into the child, rather than responding to children's cues, can instil long-term negative eating attitudes and behaviour in children.

Non-organic failure to thrive (NOFT)

Children under 2, who do not grow at the expected rate and have no underlying medical reason for this, are classified as having NOFT. The underlying reasons for NOFT are almost always psychological, social or economic. Causes include the factors previously discussed that prevent a mother/main caregiver supporting the attachment process. The condition can occur in all social classes but is more prevalent in families living in poverty where there is a chaotic family lifestyle and a history of deprivation in the parents' childhoods (Oates, 1984). Block et al. (2005: 1235) consider children born in the following situations to be at particular risk:

▸ parental depression, stress, marital strife, divorce

▸ parental history of abuse as a child

- learning difficulties and psychological abnormalities in the parent(s)

- young and single mothers without social supports

- domestic violence

- alcohol or other substance abuse

- previous child abuse in the family

- social isolation and/or poverty

- parents with inadequate adaptive and social skills

- parents who are overly focused on career and/or activities away from home

- failure to adhere to medical regimes

- lack of knowledge of normal growth and development

- infant with low birth weight or prolonged hospitalization.

Treatment is always multidisciplinary, since to treat the child as just having a nutritional disorder is unlikely to be effective. It can require the involvement of a pediatrician, nutritionist, social worker, physical or occupational therapist, and a psychiatrist or other qualified mental health provider. Without skilled intervention the future development of these children is compromised as they are at increased risk of having difficulties with learning and social and emotional development.

Non-organic failure to thrive can be a sign of child abuse and as such all early years practitioners should be aware of the condition and should follow their local child safeguarding procedures if they have concerns about an infant's welfare.

Eating disorders

Some of you may consider that a discussion about eating disorders, normally associated with adolescents and adults, is inappropriate in a text designed for early years practitioners. However, it has been suggested that the age of children with eating disorders appears to be dropping to the extent that it has been reported in 6-year-olds (Goldin, 2007). Therefore knowledge of the condition and the signs to look out for are important. In addition, we also have a responsibility for the health of the childcare workforce, which is predominantly female, some of whom will have eating disorders or problems with food and eating. Not only is this a concern for their health and well-being, but young children can be adversely affected if someone with whom they have a close relationship and spend many hours, has personal anxieties about food and body size. Managers and colleagues should be able to recognize when someone they work with has an eating disorder in order to provide sensitive support.

'Eating disorder' is the general name given to several conditions that are characterized by individuals expressing dissatisfaction with their body shape who make a conscious decision to restrict their food intake (Robinson, 2000).

Reflection point

‣ Are you satisfied with your body shape?

‣ Have you ever tried to diet to reduce your weight or exercise to tone up ready for summer?

‣ Have you sometimes found it difficult to resist the temptation to finish up the pudding in the fridge?

Most of us have, but this does not mean that we have an eating disorder. What do you think is the difference between someone who diets to look good for a wedding and someone who has an eating disorder?

The Royal College of Psychiatrists (2004) explains that the difference between wanting to be the correct weight for height and an eating disorder is that for people with an eating disorder, worries about weight become an **obsession.**

The three conditions that are generally considered to fall within the category of eating disorders are:

1 *Anorexia nervosa*: someone with anorexia nervosa is preoccupied with losing weight. They often have a distorted image of their body size, believing themselves to be overweight when the evidence is to the contrary. As a result they eat very little and, if they are female, their periods stop (RCOP, 2004).

2 *Bulimia Nervosa*: in bulimia nervosa individuals also worry about their weight, but they alternate between eating very little and bingeing on food. Bulimics often take laxatives or vomit after meals as a way of losing weight (RCOP, 2004).

3 *Binge eating*: binge eaters are usually obese and periodically indulge in massive episodes of overeating, but do not take any measures such as vomiting or laxatives to counteract the effect of bingeing (Robinson, p., 2000).

The group at highest risk of having an eating disorder is young females between the ages of 15 and 30. There is generally a ratio of 1 male to 10–20 females with an eating disorder, with anorexia nervosa being more prevalent in the higher social groups and bulimia being more evenly spread between social classes (Robinson, 2000). In relation to children under 18, the number admitted to hospital for treatment for eating disorders has risen by over a third in the past decade, with 58 children under 10 admitted for treatment in 2005–6 (Mental Health Foundation, 2007).

But what should make us think that a child or colleague has an eating disorder? The Royal College of Psychiatrists (2004) suggests the following signs are sometimes seen, although it is often very difficult to tell the difference between ordinary dieting and an eating disorder:

▸ weight loss or unusual weight changes

▸ missing meals, eating very little or avoiding 'fattening foods'

▸ avoiding eating in public, secret eating

▸ large amounts of food disappearing from cupboards

▸ believing they are fat when underweight

▸ exercising excessively

▸ becoming preoccupied with food, cooking for other people

▸ going to the bathroom or toilet immediately after meals

▸ using laxatives and vomiting to control weight.

Bryant-Waugh and Lask (1995) noted that very young children with disordered eating patterns sometimes present themselves differently from adolescents with anorexia nervosa or bulimia nervosa. In young children signs of eating disorder can include selective eating, food refusal and food avoidance. Marchi and Cohen (1990) have identified several food-associated behaviours that are predictive of children being diagnosed with an eating disorder in later childhood/ adolescence. These behaviours included:

▸ struggles over meals making mealtimes unpleasant

▸ smallness of amount eaten

▸ picky/fussy eating

▸ slowness in eating

Individuals with eating disorders will almost certainly have health-related problems. In Chapter 2 we investigated the effects on the body if an individual does not get sufficient nutrients or is obese. In addition, the RCOP (2004) suggests that an eating disorder may cause tiredness, lack of concentration, anxiety, depression, obsessive behaviour and perfectionism. There may be a lack of confidence leading to a withdrawal from friends and a dependency or over-involvement with parents instead of developing independence. Ultimately, severe eating disorders are life-threatening conditions, having one of the highest mortality rates (15 to 20 per cent) for psychiatric conditions (Tidy, 2007).

Some people are more at risk of developing an eating disorder than others. Risk factors include being previously overweight and lacking in self-esteem, being sensitive and anxious, and coming from over-protective families that find it difficult to deal with change and conflict (RCOP, 2004).

It would seem that children pick up ideas about ideal body shapes from the media and this contributes to feelings of inadequacy if their body shape fails to live up to the ideal. Pine (2001) in a study of 140 children aged 5–11 found that girls related femininity to thinness, and that by 9 years of age some girls admitted to dieting even though they were of normal height for weight.

But we should remember that ideas about body shape are culturally constructed. In her research looking at rural Jamaican constructions of food and the body, Sobo (1997) found that being a 'big man' or a 'big woman' denotes being on good terms with other people, as sharing food is linked to having good relationships, nurturance and fertility. Thus, 'people on good terms with others are large (*and*) weight loss signals social neglect' (Sobo, 1997: 257). Thus, the plumpness that comes from social eating has a different meaning for rural Jamaicans when juxtaposed with the preoccupation of thinness in urban America, for instance (Sobo, 1997). Both are examples of efforts made by individuals to construct an identity as desirable in some way, according to the particular cultural context within which they are embedded. The next chapter looks at culture and identity in relation to food and eating in more depth.

There is also a strong relationship between an individual's attachment relationships and eating disorders. Ward et al. (2001) identified that women with anorexia were more likely to have insecure attachment relationships with their mothers than women without anorexia, which could be traced back to the mothers themselves being insecurely attached as infants.

There is no single cure for eating disorders. Most young people are treated using a multidisciplinary approach involving psychotherapy or counselling, creative therapies such as art, play and dance therapy, family therapy and group therapy (GOSHT, www.ich.ucl.ac.uk).

Promoting positive attitudes towards food in early years settings

In this chapter we have looked at various theories, relating to physiological and psychological processes that influence eating behaviour. In this section we investigate the implications for practice.

The key to effective early feeding experiences appears to lie in the emotional well-being of the infant. Therefore establishing a sense of positive well-being in children whilst in early years settings should be the cornerstone of effective practice (Manning-Morton and Thorp, 2003). First and foremost there should be an effective key person structure within the setting. This involves allocating children to a named early years practitioner who has responsibility for the care of the children when they are in the setting (Goldschmeid and Jackson, 2002). A key-person relationship gives the child and carer the opportunity and time to get to know each other really well, so that a sensitive, responsive relationship can be built up, encouraging the child to become attached to the key person.

The establishment of good links with the child's parents/main caregiver is essential for the key-person relationship, as the relationship will be with the family, not just the child (Manning-Morton and Thorp, 2003). An infant who perceives that his/her parent is at ease with the setting and trusts the key person is much more likely to settle. The initial meetings with the parent/caregiver, which are opportunities to exchange information and details about how and what the child eats, are an important part of this. The key person needs to know, not only dietary restrictions, likes and dislikes, but also more intimate things such as how infants normally communicate if they are hungry and thirsty. If they are very young and being bottle-fed, how does the mother/caregiver hold the child? What routines have been built up, what songs/rhymes are used? In the early days in the setting, familiar routines will help a child settle, giving the key person and the child time to develop gradually their own routines.

It goes without saying that babies should be fed by their key person, not at a time convenient for the setting, but when the infants communicate that they are hungry. This is likely to be predictable, as infants should have developed a pattern at home. However, as we have seen, some babies are unsettled and may not yet be in a predictable pattern. The manager of the setting has a responsibility to ensure that the key person is supported by providing time, space and a peaceful atmosphere so that the infant and practitioner can relax and enjoy the feeding experience. Of course, in the early days, babies may not settle, and no one should underestimate the stress involved for the key person. In the same way that the key person needs to become attuned to the needs of the infant, the manager should be attuned to the needs of the key person and offer support (Eliot, 2007).

For older children who are starting to feed themselves, the key person should sit and eat her/his meal with their key children. Children should be encouraged to be independent and feed themselves if they want to, although it must be remembered that some children are used to being fed for longer than usual when compared to other children and no negativity should be expressed. Children will tend to copy each other and will soon be trying to feed themselves. The same advice is relevant for the use of cutlery, as in some homes children will have been trained to eat neatly with their right hand, a skill in its own right. No comment should be made if the children want to eat with their hands; it may not be long before they experiment with the cutlery that is provided.

It is important to be realistic about the behaviour you expect from children at meal-times (Manning-Morton and Thorp, 2003). Toddlers will be unable to sit for very long so it is wise to have the table set up and the food ready (not too hot) before the toddlers are invited to sit down. It is also inappropriate to ask them to remain sitting whilst the others are finishing their meals, so they should be allowed to leave the table whilst explaining to older children that they are leaving the table because they are not able to sit for very long.

The meal-time situation should be relaxed and something that the children and key person look forward to. It is best if children sit down and are served at the table, rather than having to line up with trays, even children of 5 or 6 find this daunting. They should be asked what they want to eat, and encouraged just to taste a food that they do not like. It often takes several tastes of a new food before a child likes it. Just tasting a new food should be rewarded with praise.

Practitioners should be careful about their reactions to the food being served. Children are very observant and will copy adults' behaviour, so if you are presented with food you do not like then be truthful and tell the children but also explain that you will taste a little bit in the same way that you expect them just to taste the food. Any comments about certain foods being fattening or that you are on a diet are not appropriate when you are sharing a meal with young children. This is where an observant manager or colleague may be able to pick up if a practitioner has issues about food and could have an eating disorder.

Children should be encouraged to take a small quantity of food that they think they can eat all of, rather than taking, or being given, big quantities that will be left (Greenman and Stonehouse, 1997). There should not be any compulsion to finish their first course before they get pudding as this gives the message that sweet things are a reward, or better than savoury foods.

Apart from ensuring that meal-times are enjoyable, social and stress-free, the well-being of children can be promoted throughout the day. An important aspect of this is promoting a sense of identity and self-esteem in children, as this will protect them from negative feelings about themselves that may lead to eating disorders. A full discussion about this is not possible in this text, but the recommended reading at the end of the chapter will help develop your understanding further.

Reflection point

If you are working in an early years setting, observe how meal-times are organized for children. Is it a social time that is enjoyed by all or is it fraught with tension? Are the children being given 'hidden' messages about food?

Summary

▸ Our eating behaviour is influenced by both physiological and psychological mechanisms.

▸ Obesity in children has been linked to increased impulsivity and there is a positive correlation with ADHD.

▸ Chronic stress can send out messages that the body needs foods of high calorific density, and if we are stressed we may put on more weight than unstressed individuals even if we consume the same number of calories.

▸ Children who are insecurely attached may fail to thrive and go on to have eating disorders as adults.

▸ Eating disorders have been diagnosed in children as young as 6.

▸ Positive attitudes towards eating can be promoted in early years settings by enhancing children's well-being and providing enjoyable, social and stress-free meal-times.

Discussion points

▸ Non-organic failure to thrive is often taken as a sign that a child may be being abused. At the other extreme we hear of children who are obese being put on the 'at risk' register. Do you consider that obese children should be subjected to child safeguarding proceedings?

▸ If a manager suspects that an early years practitioner in her setting has an eating disorder, how much responsibility does she have towards that member of staff and the children? How might children be affected?

Further reading

Department for Education and Skills (DfES) (2007) *Effective Practice, Key Person.* Early Years Foundation Stage resources. London: DfES.

Manning-Morton, J. and Thorp, M. (2003) *Key Times for Play: The First Three Years*. Maidenhead: Open University Press.

Satter, E. (1992) 'The feeding relationship', *Zero to Three Journal*.

Useful web sites

www.slideshare.net/medical/ns12-motivation/ (accessed 28 July 2007).

A slide show on factors that influence eating behaviour.

www.zerotothree.org/site/PageServer?pagename=ter_key_health_satter&AddInterest=1147 (accessed 28 July 2007).

www.standards.dfes.gov.uk/eyfs/resources/downloads/2_4_ep.pdf

Great Ormond St Hospital Trust (2007) www.ich.ucl.ac.uk/factsheets/children/C070009/(accessed 4 December 2007).

Food, Culture and Identity

The focus in this chapter is on the symbolic importance of food and eating, and its role in constructing individuals' identities. Here, food and eating are explored in terms of their cultural significance as opposed to their nutritional importance. The chapter also explores the multiple and shifting meanings food and eating have in human lives. Finally, religion, ethnicity, ethical consumerism, class, gender and children's **agency** in relation to food and eating are considered, including a discussion of children's sweet-eating.

So far in this book, we have looked at food and eating in terms of nutrition, health inequalities and emotion. Whilst these approaches are important in terms of individual children's physical and emotional health, as well as the material conditions that impact upon health inequalities, food and eating have a symbolic significance that goes beyond these areas. This chapter aims to look at this, drawing primarily upon **structuralist** and **post-structuralist** writing in this area. The key areas that are explored in the chapter are:

▸ The symbolic significance of food and eating

▸ Food, identity and religion

▸ Food, identity and ethnicity

▸ Food, identity and the 'green' or ethical consumer perspective

▸ Food, identity and class

▸ Food, identity and gender

▸ Children becoming part of the wider world.

The symbolic significance of food and eating

Structuralist approaches to food and eating, which come primarily from **social anthropology**, tend to see taste as socially controlled and culturally shaped

(Caplan, 1997). Levi-Strauss (1966), a particularly important writer in this area, argues that societies reveal their hidden structure through food. In other words, food is seen as a code or a symbolic language (Barthes, 1975).

Structuralist approaches to food and eating may focus upon what people eat in different societies and the ways in which food acts as a marker of special occasions and the 'rhythm' of the year. This rhythm can be seen in the way that there are cultural approaches to fasting and feasting, often linked to religious festivals, as well as foods linked to celebrations, such as birthday cakes. This rhythm can also be seen in the way many societies structure their days and weeks around certain foods (Delamont, 1995). Some of you may be familiar with eating breakfast, dinner and tea at certain times of the day; you may have particular ideas around what constitutes a 'proper' meal; and you may eat particular foods on particular days, such as fish on a Friday or a roast dinner on a Sunday.

The idea that food and eating occupy a symbolic order can also be seen in the work of Mary Douglas (1997). Murcott (1988) describes Douglas's work as important because she focuses on how the act of cooking and eating food is one of the many family systems, which are culturally determined, for servicing the body. Importantly, Douglas argues that the pattern of meal-times and the structure of individual meals are important because the minutiae of everyday life have fundamental meaning for human beings (Murcott, 1988).

Reflection point

Think about your own experience of food and eating. Can you see a pattern in the way you eat foods over a day, week and year? How aware are you of the typical eating patterns of the children and families you work with?

Unlike structuralist approaches to food and eating, post-structuralist approaches favour a notion of multiple and shifting meanings, meanings attached to a shifting sense of identity according to context, which includes power relations within that context (Albon, 2005; Mennell et al., 1992). The term 'subjectivity' is often used in post-structuralist writing as it highlights the many ways people come to understand themselves as individuals and how they experience their lives (Lupton, 1996).

The notion of identity, then, is an important concept in relation to food and eating. Our identities are inextricably bound up with what we eat as we, quite literally, are what we eat (Falk, 1991; Lupton, 1994), unlike other aspects of material culture, such as clothing, which remain external to the body (Meigs, 1997). For Giddens (1991), individuals, in what he describes as the late modern period, are constantly engaged in constructing their own identities. Consumption, of which food is a part, plays a critical role in the formation of these identities because as Valentine (1999: 491) maintains, 'Goods can be used to locate ourselves within narratives which are not of our own making – electing us to a shared form of identification and because they help us to construct and maintain individual narratives of the self.'

Consumption can be viewed as linked to self-identity. Baudrillard uses the term 'signifiers' to denote the way that products take on the meanings we ascribe to them as distinct from their actual utility (Jagger, 2000). Here, we might think about the way foods are packaged in order to appeal to young children, using characters from popular culture to encourage children to identify with, and ultimately encourage their parents to buy, certain products. The packaging encourages a sense of identification with the product, which goes beyond merely eating the food, aiming to persuade the consumer to identify with the product in other ways. An example might be encouraging children to think that they will have more friends if they eat certain products.

Reflection point

In order to think further about food and eating as having multiple and shifting meanings, try to think about a practical example. Think about a particular food – say, biscuits. Eating those biscuits may mean something very different according to the time and place you eat them in, the people you eat them with, the way you are feeling, and so on. In other words, their meaning is not fixed.

▸ Eating the biscuits may signify a special occasion, which is shared with close friends and family, such as a birthday.

▸ Eating the biscuits may break up the boredom of a meeting at work.

▸ Eating the biscuits may be comforting after a long day at work, when you are snuggled on the sofa.

▸ Eating the biscuits may be a quick energy boost when you are busy at work and need to eat something when you are on the move.

▸ Eating the biscuits may remind you of particular people, places and events – something individual to you.

▸ Eating the biscuits may make you feel guilty as they are unlikely to be considered a healthy eating option – you may even hide the fact you have eaten them!

▸ Eating the biscuits may make you feel sophisticated, or similar, because the packaging and advertising promotes an image of luxury and pleasure

(Continued)

(Continued)

You can imagine many more possible meanings that these biscuits might conjure to an individual, but these are various and shifting. In addition, you might imagine that if someone, say a female colleague, in the second example ate a lot of biscuits and did not share them with colleagues, she would be censored in some way as she may have ignored unwritten, cultural rules about the sharing of food. This may be exacerbated by cultural conceptions about the way women are expected to develop and maintain a particular body shape. In this sense we can see how power is exercised through food – a key concept in relation to post-structuralism. Foucault (1977) describes this as 'technologies of the self' to denote the ways in which individuals internalize rules of behaviour and emotions, and use these in their everyday lives, often unthinkingly.

So far in this chapter, we have argued that food and eating play an important role in our sense of identity. What follows is further discussion of food and identity, exploring the issue in terms of religion, ethnicity, a 'green' or ethical consumer perspective, class and gender. In reading through the following sections, it is important to keep in mind the intersection of these different aspects of our identity, as all may be important in impacting on our food and eating practices.

Food, identity and religion

As many of you are aware, there are particular taboos regarding some foods, which are linked to religion. In relation to early childhood practice, it is important that early years practitioners are aware of, and sensitive to, people's different food and eating patterns based on these (Lindon, 2006). However, it is also important to ensure that practitioners do not make assumptions as to what people eat or do not eat purely on the basis of this. Individuals may well have their own variations on what they eat or do not eat; some families may follow religious guidance strictly and others less so. Therefore, it is imperative that early years practitioners discuss food and eating practices in detail with individual families to ensure that mistakes are not made. Table 6.1 outlines some of the main areas that early years practitioners need to be aware of in relation to religious observances around some foods.

As can be seen from the table, early years practitioners need to be aware, not only about the foods they prepare for young children, but also the ways in which they serve these foods. Food and eating practices may change according

Table 6.1 Food and religion

Religion	Foods likely not to be eaten	Other issues and things to check
Islam	Pork and all pork products. Other meats, including poultry, must be halal, which means lawful. This involves the animal being slaughtered in the accepted way and dedicated to Allah by the Imam	Check how strictly Muslim families adhere to particular dietary practices. Some families may not eat foods containing particular food additives. In some instances, the local mosque will provide guidance about this. During the four weeks of Ramadan, Muslims fast from dawn until dusk in order to show their ability to focus on Islamic spiritual standards. It is very unlikely that young children or pregnant women would be expected to fast, but older Muslim children and adults may be fasting. If Ramadan falls during the summer months, in particular, fasting individuals may feel tired as they will have risen before dawn to pray and have their pre-dawn meal, and it may be some time until the sun goes down and food can be eaten again
Judaism	Pork and probably no shellfish. For Jewish people, who follow dietary practices strictly, all meat must be kosher that is, the way butchers kill animals – it must be done according to the accepted method and involves a blessing by the Rabbi	Dairy products have to be kept separate from meat products during food preparation, serving, eating and clearing up/washing up. For those families who follow the laws of the Kashrut strictly, that is, the dietary laws, kitchens need to be organized on kosher lines. If the kitchen in your setting is not organized on kosher lines, this might mean that children bring in a packed lunch. Some Jewish families will fast on the evening prior to Yom Kippur until the next evening (during festival of Rosh Hashanah)
Hinduism	Beef and beef products. Some Hindus are vegetarian	You should note that there are many variations to dietary practice
Sikhism	Beef and beef products and possibly pork. Some Sikhs are vegetarian	

(Continued)

Table 6.1 (Continued)

Religion	Foods likely not to be eaten	Other issues and things to check
Christianity	Generally, there are no hard and fast rules about food and drink	Some Christian groups may have different practices, for example, Jehovah's Witnesses may require that meat has been bled during slaughter Some Christians avoid meat on a Friday as it was the day when Christ died Some Christians may give up some foods during Lent, in the lead-up to Easter, for example, sugar, or if from the Orthodox Church tradition, may avoid dairy products, eggs and meat products during Lent
Rastafarianism (a form of Christianity)	Pork, shellfish, sometimes dairy products are not eaten.	Strict followers of Rastafarianism may not eat or drink processed foods such as bottled orange juice, preferring to squeeze juice from the fruit itself
Buddhism	Sometimes vegetarian	If vegetarian, practitioners may need to check whether products contain animal-derived ingredients such as gelatine or rennet, which might be found in jelly, ice cream or cheese respectively. There are vegetarian equivalents

to the particular time in which they are eaten, for instance, during times of religious fasting (Lindon, 2006). To reiterate a previous point, what is essential is that we do not make assumptions about what people do and do not eat based on their religion. How religious dietary practices manifest themselves in one country or region may differ elsewhere and there may be individual differences around people's diets, not least how strictly individuals observe religious teachings.

Activity

Find out more about religious observances in relation to food and drink on the web site below:

www.faqs.org/nutrition/Pre-Sma/Religion-and-Dietary-Practices.html

Food, identity and ethnicity

Ethnicity may be important in relation to food choice. Whilst it almost seems a truism that people of different national and regional distinctions are likely to eat different things, based on what grows in the area and what religious and cultural practices have developed in that area, globalization, immigration and emigration have impacted upon the foods people eat. As people have moved around the globe, there is a very real sense in which food is a means by which people maintain a particular cultural identity and adapt to a new environment.

What is defined as a food is, itself, a social construction (Meigs, 1997). By this we mean that what is considered edible or not, and the meanings ascribed to certain foods, are situated within a particular culture and a particular point in time. Different foods are attributed with different meanings, which encompass what Counihan and Van-Esterik (1997: 3) describe as including both the 'material and magical'. An example of this can be seen in Meigs's (1997) research with the Hua people in the East Highlands of Papua New Guinea. Different properties are ascribed to different foods and according to who prepares the food and the consumer of it. For instance, there are strict rules around the foods a parent can give to their children, and vice versa. Food, in this community, is imbued with a mystical quality, one that acts to bind the community together.

For some Black American women writers, what is known as 'soul-food' is linked to a search for cultural identity. Hughes argues,

> The essence of Black culture has been handed down through oral history, generation after generation in the African tradition, through the

selection and preparation of soul food. The dominant figure in the cultural translation through food is the Black woman. Her expressions of
love, nurturance, creativity, sharing, patience, economic frustration, survival, and the very core of her African heritage are embodied in her meal
preparation. (Hughes, 1997: 272)

By soul food, Hughes is talking about roots and seeds of plants brought over to
America from Africa. These would include watermelon, black-eyed peas and okra.
Hughes (1997) argues that these seeds are symbolic of the struggle of Black people to preserve their culture, both externally and internally through food, when
forced to leave Africa into slavery. In addition to this, soul food denotes freshly
cooked food, which is likely to include meats such as chitterlings and the parts of
an animal often thrown away, but utilized as an economic necessity by Black
people alongside an array of greens. Recipes for particular soul food dishes were
handed down orally from mother to daughter and the kitchen was central as the
social hub of the home. Later in this chapter, we see that gender is a crucially
important factor in any discussion of food and eating.

The importance of maintaining a sense of one's cultural identity through food
is important, especially to people who have migrated to a new country. Many
of you reading this book will have personal and/or professional experience of
this, either through moving to a new country or region yourselves or in working with families who have experienced this. In Jonsson et al.'s (2002) research
into Somalian women's experience of food and eating on migrating to Sweden,
they found women oscillating between wishing to become part of the Swedish
community and maintaining their cultural identity as Somalian. They argue,
'When coming to a new country, everyday food choice becomes an ethnic act
made evident when meeting the food of the host community' (Jonsson et al.,
2002: 328). This can be seen in the Somalian women's 'longing for cultural
taste'; a taste that is permeated with the 'cultural identity one longs for in exile'
(Jonsson et al., 2002: 333). This was especially evident in the feeding of their
children. The Somalian women in the study believed maintaining their Somalian
dietary practices was essential in their children's development of a strong
Somalian cultural identity. These women experienced difficulties when their
children were in school or a childcare setting because their children were having at least one meal a day in that setting – a meal that reflected Swedish rather
than Somalian cuisine. Many foods, such as sorghum and camel meat, were
unavailable to these women, and traditional Somalian forms of food preparation were juxtaposed with the Swedish preoccupation with 'easy meals'. In
addition, the research pointed to the way that food and spices play an important role in Somalian culture as prescriptions for a range of cures, such as
using a mixture of sesame or olive oil and lemon juice as a massage oil for children with a cough. Traditional foods and spices, used as home treatments, such
as black cumin, were sometimes hard to source in Sweden.

Activity

If you have had personal experience of moving to a new country or region, think about the extent to which it was important for you to be able to eat familiar foods. If you have not had this experience, try to talk to people who have and find out which foods they particularly miss and why these were, or are, the foods they pine for especially.

You might like to read the children's story *Grandma's Saturday Soup*, written by Sally Fraser and Derek Brazell (published in 2005 by Mantra Lingua). It is a story about a child who misses her grandma and every day sees reminders of her grandma's wonderful Saturday Soup as well as grandma herself and her Jamaican heritage.

There seems to be little written about the experience of Black and minority ethnic (BME) groups that have emigrated to Britain in terms of their eating experiences (Caplan, 1997). Whilst we should not assume that people eat particular foods based purely on their ethnicity or religion, food and eating are likely to play an important role in people's maintenance of a particular cultural identity (Caplan, 1994). Bradby's (1997) study of Glaswegian Punjabi women's perspectives on food and eating highlights how these women classified foods into 'your foods' and 'our foods' as well as constructed narratives around particular foods in order to justify eating them. Ghee, for instance, was reported as being 'good for your insides … and your bones' because it provides lubrication … important if suffering from constipation or during childbirth' (Bradby, 1997: 227). The women in the study were concerned with whether foods contributed to their health, or not, and used medical wisdom, with its associated descriptions as to how a particular food is beneficial to a particular part of the body. Alternatively, these women also drew upon a systemic or **Ayurvedic** model from the advice of elders, which looks at the merits of particular foods according to their ability to keep the body in some sort of balance or equilibrium. Bradby's study highlights the importance of thinking about how messages about healthy eating are taken up according to the cultural beliefs of different groups.

Finally, in this section, it is important to consider the impact migration has had on the food and eating practices of countries and regions. Whilst in quizzes we might be asked to associate foods with particular countries or regions, such as goulash with Hungary, in reality such a fixed stereotype around the foods we eat does not hold up (James, 1997). The impact of migration on the foods eaten in particular countries can be seen in the way that cuisines have developed over time. Recipes are 'invented and reinvented from different cultures and regions of the world' (Wright et al., 2001: 354), an example of which is the Indian Balti, which Wright et al. (2001) observe was invented in Birmingham as opposed to a city in India.

As James (1997) observes, there is a huge diversity of food eaten in any given society. However, she stresses that the continuance of stereotypes of national or regional cuisines still forms the basis of people's encounters with foreign foods: 'Indeed, food is one of the primary ways in which notions of "otherness" are articulated' (James, 1997: 72).

Reflection point

Think about James's quotation above and consider the number of times you hear people commenting on what *we* eat and what *they* eat. Think about how such language serves to include some people and exclude others.

In addition, reflect on Wright et al.'s (2001) assertion that in Britain there seems to be a fragmentation of tastes that transcends national borders – a position that points to a more complex view of food and taste.

Food, identity and the 'green' or ethical consumer perspective

So far we have looked at the intersection of religion and ethnicity and food in terms of individual identity, because identity is bound up with what we eat and what we do not eat. However, these are not the only factors that impact on food choice. For some people, this is an ethical issue as it links to broader issues of consumption, which might include:

▶ the way animals are reared and killed

▶ the way live animals are transported

▶ the increased use of pesticides and technologies such as the genetic modification (GM) of foods

▶ the impact of transporting food over long distances on global warming, when it could be grown and delivered locally

▶ global capitalism and the way small producers and suppliers, some of whom are in majority world countries, do not see a fair share of the profits of their labour.

This is certainly not meant to be an exhaustive list, but it does go some way to show that people's consumption patterns are linked to a range of complex issues. Within what we might call the 'green' or ethical consumer perspective on food and eating, some individuals construct a particular sense of identity from avoiding and eating certain foods, such as:

▸ eating locally grown produce, possibly even growing their own

▸ eating organically grown foods and avoiding GM foods

▸ becoming vegetarian or vegan

▸ eating free-range produce

▸ buying fair-trade products

▸ thinking what happens to waste, such as recycling and composting.

In buying and eating certain foods instead of others, people construct and maintain a particular identity – here, that of being an ethical consumer. Giddens (1991: 215) might refer to this as 'life-politics' as it involves making political decisions about how to construct one's self-identity. Crucially, though, Giddens (1991) maintains that in order to make such lifestyle choices, a person needs to be in the material and political position to make them. This is of fundamental importance. You may recall that Chapter 4 of this book highlighted how poverty is linked directly to food inequalities and subsequent poor health.

Fiddes (1997: 252) sees the growth in vegetarianism as a 'widening of the ethical net'. For writers such as Singer (1975), the oppression of animals is described as 'speciesism' as non-human animals are afforded fewer rights than humans. Speciesism is likened to Black and minority ethnic people's experience of racism and women's experience of sexism. Women, in particular, seem to be drawn to vegetarianism, possibly as a rejection of meat's association with images of masculinity (Wright et al., 2001).

Importantly, some early childhood settings have worked hard to develop a more ethical approach to food and eating as part of a wider ethical perspective on practice, such as using real nappies instead of disposable ones. In relation to food and eating, they have tried to source local food suppliers, grow their own foods and recycle food waste, for instance.

Food, identity and class

The impact of poverty on people's food and eating was explored in depth in Chapter 4, which looked at health inequalities around food. This short section explores the impact of class on food and eating from a different perspective, drawing especially on the work of Pierre Bourdieu.

Bourdieu (1986) believes that economic differences are not the sole reason why people of different classes eat different things. He maintains that there is an unconscious cultural reproduction of taste from one generation to the next, something he describes as 'habitus'. From birth, according to Bourdieu, children are socialized into particular tastes, such as liking sweet foods. These tastes are elaborated over generations.

James (1997) argues that something more subtle is happening to consumption habits. She maintains that in the past, a marker of class difference in Britain was the preference of middle-class people for eating 'foreign' foods, notably French food. This marked them out as distinct from working-class people, who ate more simply, relying on traditional British foods. More recent food trends, she suggests, point to class distinction in food being perpetuated in cooking and eating traditional British foods as opposed to the easily available cuisines from India, China and southern Europe. As increasing numbers of people from all social classes are eating a wide variety of regional, national and global cuisines, middle-class people seem to be preserving their class distinction through cooking and eating traditional British foods.

If we think back to the earlier discussion about food, identity and ethnicity, we might wish to be cautious about making links between class background and food preferences. Globalization, for instance, has had a profound impact on the foods we eat and our 'tastes' for particular foods may not have their basis purely in class or ethnicity (Wright et al., 2001).

Food, identity and gender

A consideration of gender in relation to food and identity is of central importance. Already, this chapter has drawn upon research in this area. Much of the literature around food and eating focuses on gender, the reasons for which might include the following:

▸ Pregnant and breastfeeding mothers are expected to think carefully about the foods they eat in order to ensure the continued health of their babies.

▸ It is women, not men, who are able to produce food in the form of milk – thus women, as mothers, have an embodied experience of food as *producers* of food, feeding their babies with their own bodies.

▸ Women, especially mothers, are subject to a great deal of child-rearing literature, much of which focuses upon feeding the family.

▸ Women tend to have prime responsibility for shopping, preparing, cooking and serving food.

▸ There is an expectation that women, as mothers, will help their children to develop culturally expected, socially acceptable food and eating habits.

Fischler's (1988) research focuses specifically on gender. He maintains that food preparation and provisioning often falls to women and they are also expected to account for individual preferences within their families. The way food operates in families, but in particular the intersection of gender within families, is a crucial one. Mennell et al. (1992) point out the difficulties women experience when feeding male partners alongside children. They argue that for women, feeding their children involves loving and pleasing their children as well as their partner. This also means acquiescing to their children's demands for particular foods, inculcating cultural ideas around good manners, as well as acting as guardians of their families' health (Charles and Kerr, 1986; Ekstrom, 1991).

Some of you may have worked with young children who are obese, and their families. In your discussions with the child's family, you may well have come across the complex issues that underpin the child's obesity and the family's approach to food and eating. Whilst a parent may know that it would be better for their child to eat fruit instead of sweets and crisps, they may continue to give their child sweets and crisps because, amongst other things, the parent derives satisfaction from giving their child something that they enjoy and will eat. Furthermore, the decisions women make about food cannot be understood purely in terms of nutrition; they may give their children snacks in order to facilitate shopping and preparing food safely and with few distractions (Murphy et al., 1998).

Feeding a family, it would seem, is a complex issue; one where issues of power, influence and control impact upon women. This is often played out via male partners' views around 'proper eating' and what it means to be a 'good wife and mother' (McIntosh and Zey, 1989).

Reflection point

Do you have a particular view of what constitutes a 'proper meal'? What would it include? You will note that we use inverted commas around 'proper meal' to denote how this is a social construction and may be understood differently by different people.

Where do these ideas come from? Do you make negative judgements about parents, particularly mothers, who do not feed their children a 'proper meal' regularly, that is, according to your definition of a 'proper meal'?

In thinking about what constitutes a 'proper meal' and ideas about how this links to notions of being a 'good wife and mother', as McIntosh and Zey (1989) put it, women too are engaged in reinforcing such ideas. In Mitchell and Green's (2002) study, many mothers highlighted their own success as mothers by distancing themselves from 'Other' mothers, who are characterized as uncaring or bad mothers. By juxtaposing their own situation with that of 'Other' mothers, the mothers in the study were able to foster a positive self-identity. However, the corollary of this is that a **Foucaultian** system of self-surveillance seems to operate. This 'Othering' of mothers, whose child-rearing practices are perceived as different and inferior to their own, serves to reinforce increased control over what it is to be a good mother in society as a whole.

This can be seen further when we consider what it means to be a 'good mother'. Wallbank (2001) argues that this incorporates the idea that mothers should meet all their children's needs. In Albon's (2003; 2006) research into sweet-eating in families, mothers expressed concern over 'Other' families' practices around sweet-eating, which served to reinforce the prevailing discourse around good parenting. Julie, a parent in the study, commented in the following way about her friend Sharon's sweet-buying:

> She buys her kids all these horrible sweets. I'd never buy him (*her son*) them, but it's really hard when you're sharing a lift with her and she buys all her kids the same sweets so they don't argue – she gets him the same as them, but I wouldn't buy them. Apart from anything else they're a waste of money and are full of E numbers and all that. Sharon gets her kids whatever sweet they want. They sit in the car and dish out their orders before she drops them off at school and whatever they've been like, she lets them have the sweets – they remember what they've said at the end of the day and there's arguments if they don't get them. I'd never let him (*nodding towards her son*) tell me what to do like that. It's caused some problems between us – in fact I try not to get in the car with her as often as I used to. (Albon, 2003: 57)

In your work with young children and families, you may well have come across food and eating practices that are different from your own, that may challenge your thinking and that of your team. You may well have found yourself commenting negatively on some of the following instances, in a similar way to the parent quoted above:

- a child in a Reception class, who has never used a knife and fork
- a child who comes to nursery eating a bag of crisps as he/she has not had time for breakfast
- a toddler or young child who is allowed to move around, rather than remaining seated, while eating at home
- a young child, who expects you to feed him/her, rather than manage independently
- a child who has lots of sweet foods in his/her lunch box.

Whilst some of these examples directly relate to the children's actual food intake, others relate to the way in which food is imbibed. If we are honest, there are instances when all of us, as early years practitioners, find a clash between our own personal beliefs and practices and those of the families we work with. In reflecting on the instances above, you might also like to consider whether you hold women, as mothers, primarily responsible for their children's food intake and developing culturally accepted ideas around the *way* their children eat.

Children becoming part of the wider world

Food and eating play a crucial role in the way children are inculcated into the wider world (Ben-Ari, 1997; Golden, 2005). Wessien et al.'s (2002) research highlights how each culture passes on its food patterns to the next generation. Crucially, nursery settings and parents share responsibility for socializing children into culturally accepted food norms. However, there are variations within these 'norms'. If we think of young children, as they grow older they are likely to move between an increasing range of different social worlds, each characterized by slightly different foods and different social rules governing how these foods should be eaten, albeit that these rules are often unspoken. Caplan (1997) uses the term 'food codes' in this respect. Caplan suggests, 'Food is like a language – its meaning can shift according to contexts of time and place and people can switch food codes just as they do language codes, depending on with whom they are communicating at any point in time' (Caplan, 1997: 6).

Increasingly, work in the area of food and eating is beginning to focus on children's perspectives. This is important, because, as Grieshaber (1997) notes, children are often positioned as passive recipients of food, with little acknowledgement of the ways in which they impact on the decision-making around food consumption in their families. Whilst we look again at children's perspectives on food and eating in Chapter 7, here we look at the issue of power.

Grieshaber's (1997) research looked at four families in Australia and the way that meal-time rules are constructed and maintained within them. She highlights the ways in which children are engaged in a daily cycle of struggle and resistance with their parents around food. Each family had generated its own rules around meal-times, but these were constantly being renegotiated and challenged by the children. It would seem, from research in the past ten years, that children are increasingly being viewed as social actors, impacting on household food decisions around *what* and *when* to eat (Dixon and Banwell, 2004; Robinson, 2000; Valentine, 1999).

The way we eat

Whilst *what* we eat is determined by the many ways we construct our identities, there are also cultural differences in the *way* we eat particular foods. Whilst it would be easy to ascribe this to particular ethnic groups, such as using chopsticks if belonging to a Japanese or Chinese ethnic group or using some sort of pliable food such as a chapatti to guide food into the mouth, as in some Asian and African societies (Lindon, 2006), it would be wrong to assume this is fixed. People may eat differently according to the people they are eating with or the particular occasion they are part of.

This links to the previously made point that as children get older they move between an increasing range of social worlds, each with particular rules around food and eating practices. If we think about this in relation to the *way* we eat, as opposed to the actual food we imbibe, an individual might eat a pizza in a formal manner, using a knife and fork and sitting at the table, if in a restaurant with people they do not know well. However, if they had the same pizza as a takeaway at home with family and close friends, they might eat it whilst sitting on the floor, straight from the packaging and with fingers. Even young children experience these different ways of eating and some will be familiar with using a range of implements such as fingers, spoons, knives, forks, chopsticks, and so on.

Reflection point

Look at the following abridged observation of a 4-year-old child, Emma, playing in a nursery, and reflect upon her knowledge of cultural rules around food and eating as well as different contexts for food and eating.

Emma was playing in the home corner. After a while she said 'I know, let's play takeaways' and ran to get a calculator. 'You tell me what you want and I'll get it for you – you can have anything.' Debbie telephoned in and asked Emma to get her chicken madras and naan bread. She told her 'It'll be at least an hour' and when Debbie asked how much it would cost, Emma said 'it's free' adding 'you get a free bottle of wine'. Over the next half hour, they had a whole range of different styles of takeaway – Chinese, Indian, KFC, Macdonald's, fish and chips, and so on. Each time, Emma said, 'you got to eat it like this … ' and demonstrated how each of the styles of food would be eaten – noting the ways in which it is culturally acceptable in her household to eat fish and chips, burgers, Chinese food and the like.

As Emma took down the orders with another child, she told the customer on the telephone how long it would take to cook the food and on one occasion when Debbie feigned being annoyed at the length of time it would take, said 'I'll put some prawn crackers in free for you if you like' in the style

---

(Continued)

of a waiter trying to appease a customer. She used the calculator to type in orders and used a range of different voices in the play – more colloquial when shouting through to the kitchens what the order was, for example shouting 'we need cod and chips twice'; more formal when dealing with a customer, such as 'what can I get you to eat my dear?' Emma stated that her family has a takeaway every Friday night 'when mummy doesn't like cooking'. She later reported 'We have Macdonald's on a Saturday before mummy goes to work – we have breakfast there'.

Like adults, children may choose which implements they wish to use according to the occasion – at times this will be determined for them by adults. In a nursery setting, many children aged 3 years old are expected to drink from a cup. However, at home, these same children may drink from a feeder cup or possibly a bottle, especially if close to bedtime or during the night if they wake up. There are likely to be a range of possible reasons for this, including parents' concerns around the child spilling their drink on the furniture or carpets, as well as the comforting action of drinking from a bottle. After all, it is easier to have a cuddle if drinking from a bottle than drinking from a cup and the action of sucking from the bottle is often a comforting precursor to sleeping.

Giovanni (2006) highlights the importance of nurseries in reconciling collective, cultural values with children's individual needs during meal-times. She stresses how meal-times are of prime importance as a means through which children are introduced to a sense of collective participation in the life of the nursery. A group identity is forged through the collective participation of nursery members in the rituals that develop around mealtimes.

Reflection point

Reflect on the rituals you have around food and eating in your setting. These might include singing particular songs in the lead-up to the meal, the physical layout of the tables or the way food is served and crockery cleared away.

Children and sweets

The final section in this chapter looks specifically at sweet-eating. Sweets are interesting because they are a food and a non-food and rarely play a part in meal-times (James, 1990). Moreover, Albon (2005) argues that sweets should be viewed as positioned between a food and a cultural artefact, such as the electronic games many children have.

Research with children in the North East of England, shows how they use the term 'kets' to describe the inexpensive, cheap and garish sweets they eat – 'kets' being a word that means 'rubbish' or 'useless' (James, 1998). For children, sweets are the 'metaphorical meals of childhood' (James, 1998: 402) because they are inexpensive and therefore under the child's control. Sweets may be spat out, rather than swallowed, may fizz or form bubbles and may be a colour that is unlike other foods – arguably sweets transgress what a real food should be (Albon, 2006).

Sweets, as an example of children's popular culture, seem to offer children a way into a shared experience of childhood with other children (Seiter, 1998) and as such, should be seen as situating children in a particular culture at a particular point in time (Albon, 2006). Indeed one parent in Albon's (2006: 16–17) study commented:

> Your first sweets (*said when looking at her daughter*) were probably when you were about ten months to a year – when you had your first Easter eggs … (*Alison, the parent, turns to me saying*) I've got a photo of Emma with chocolate smeared down her face. She didn't realize what was going on I suppose, but for me it was like she was taking part in the wider world – like she was a real person all of a sudden.

Dixon and Banwell (2004) point out that advertisements play an important part in forming children's views around what they want to eat. However, we should be wary about seeing children as dupes of the advertisers (Seiter, 1998). Albon's (2006) research shows how children are engaged in play-making and story-making around sweet-eating. She goes on to argue that this is very powerful for young children and should not be ignored in any discussion around healthy eating. Albon (2006) also suggests that parents, too, may be engaged in a degree of playful subversion in their roles of looking after their children's health, such as in play around bubble-gum blowing. You might like to think about the extent to which you think children are influenced by the advertising around them and how this impacts on their understandings of food and health.

Summary ☐

▸ Food and eating have a symbolic importance that goes beyond the importance of imbibing one's nutritional requirements.

‣ What we eat, and what we do not eat, play an important part in our sense of personal identity.

‣ Religion, ethnicity, the 'green' perspective, class and gender impact on the way we view certain foods and food and eating in general.

‣ Gender seems to be especially important in any discussion about food and eating – particularly the importance ascribed to women, as mothers, feeding their families.

‣ Food and eating are important to consider when thinking about how children become part of the wider world. However, children do not passively accept what adults give them; they impact on families' food choices and may be actively engaged in resisting adult rules about food.

‣ Sweet-eating is an example of children's non-conformity to adult rules about food. Alongside this, sweets play an important role in children's popular culture; this should not be ignored in any discussion about healthy eating.

Discussion points

‣ Does your setting discourage parents from bringing in cakes and sweets for birthday celebrations? If it does, reflect on the symbolic significance of birthday cakes

‣ Consider the degree to which staff in your setting make comments, positive and negative, about families based on the food families bring in from home. This might be in the form of their child's lunch-box, a gift, or food for sharing during a celebration. Reflect on the extent to which such comments relate to families' social class, for instance.

‣ Reflect on the extent to which you think rituals, such as those mentioned in the final part of the chapter, are important in early childhood practice. How can these be reconciled with meeting children's individual needs?

Further reading

Albon, D. (2006) 'Sweet memories: an examination of six families' narratives around sweet-eating', *Early Childhood Practice*, 8(1): 12–20.

Jonsson, I.M., Hallberg, L.R.-M. and Gustafsson, I.-B. (2002) 'Cultural foodways in Sweden: repeated focus group interviews with Somalian women', *International Journal of Consumer Studies*, 26(4): 328–39.

Lupton, D. (1996) *Food, the Body and the Self*. London: Sage.

Useful web sites

www.faqs.org/nutrition/Pre-Sma/Religion-and-Dietary-Practices.html

www.soilassociation.org/ (web site for the Soil Association, an environmental charity that supports sustainable, organic farming and champions human health).

(Accessed 25 July 2007)

Promoting Healthy Eating in Early Childhood Settings

This chapter discusses why promoting healthy eating is vital in early childhood settings and looks at approaches to health promotion and what these might look like in practice. In addition, the chapter considers how promoting healthy eating should be embedded in the early years curriculum, and advocates an approach where listening to children and planning for inclusion and equality is central. Finally, the chapter looks at how any programme aiming to promote healthy eating needs to involve parents and carers.

In Chapter 1 of this book we looked at the development of policy in relation to young children's food and eating. Here, we focus on one particular aspect of recent policy trends – health promotion. The move to health promotion strategies encourages early childhood practitioners to empower children with the knowledge, skills and attitudes that will enable them to make healthy choices both now and in adulthood. It is important to note early on in this chapter, that whilst the focus here is on food and eating, this is but one way that practitioners might promote the health of young children. The encouragement of regular sleep and exercise, safety in the sun, as well as toileting and washing routines, are examples of other areas which, alongside the encouragement of healthy eating, form part of a holistic approach to health promotion in early childhood settings.

This chapter aims to look at the following key areas:

▸ Why should we promote healthy eating in the early years?

▸ What do we mean by health promotion?

▸ Promoting healthy eating and the early years curriculum

▸ Listening to children

▸ Involving parents in promoting healthy eating

▸ Developing a health promotion programme.

Why should we promote healthy eating in the early years?

This book has argued that it is important to promote healthy eating from an early age – indeed, as Chapter 2 noted, a healthy diet is important for any woman hoping to conceive, as well as during pregnancy. From infancy, children are forming ideas about the world and it is generally agreed that dietary habits that are formed in childhood are often fixed in adulthood (Sellers et al., 2005). Thus, getting into good dietary habits in early childhood is vital.

Not only this, but Chapter 2 stressed how a good diet is vital for later optimum health and highlighted how a poor diet increases the likelihood of a range of illnesses. Sellers et al. (2005), for instance, highlight the importance of intervention in the early years in reducing obesity and overweight later in life.

However, there is a more immediate need for a good diet. We have also noted in this book that young children's health is affected now by their diet. The prevalence of childhood obesity is increasing and impacts on children's chances of developing type 2 diabetes. Not only this, but the quality of children's diets may also impact directly on their behaviour and their ability to learn (Dani et al., 2005).

Finally here, in some early childhood settings, unlike the majority of schools, children receive their breakfast, dinner and tea, as well as snacks, five days a week for most of the year. Therefore, early childhood settings play a significant role in ensuring that the diets of the children in their care are nutritious.

We might conclude from this that promoting healthy eating is vital in the early years. Before moving on to discuss strategies, such as how healthy eating might be embedded in the early childhood curriculum, we need to explore approaches that may be employed in health promotion.

What do we mean by health promotion?

Naidoo and Wills (2000) trace the development of the idea of health promotion from the public health measures for disease prevention in the nineteenth century to health education approaches in the twentieth century, which tended to focus on giving out information and advice. Health education approaches, as distinct from health promotion approaches, tend to be based on an 'expert authority model', where the health educator is deemed to be able to decide:

▸ what health needs someone or a group might have

▸ whether an individual's lifestyle is adequate

▸ what types of intervention should happen and how this should be communicated

▸ whether the interventions are a success or not (summarized from Naidoo and Wills, 2000: 80).

Such an approach to health can be criticized for its tendency to focus on bringing about changes to people's lifestyles based on information and persuasion to change driven by professional experts (Naidoo and Wills, 2000). Thus, empowerment has emerged as an important principle in health promotion.

Reflection point

Spend a few moments thinking about what is meant by empowerment. How might it relate to health promotion?

For Scriven and Stiddard (2003: 110), empowerment has become the 'catchword and philosophical tenet for health promotion' as, following the Ottawa Charter (WHO, 1986) mentioned in Chapter 1, it refers to the process by which people have increased control over improving their own health. In addition, health promotion should be seen as requiring a removal of any barriers to attaining optimum health for everyone. In other words there is a principle of equality that underpins health promotion (Tones, 2001). Whilst schools and, we would add, all early childhood settings are important sites for health promotion, Scriven and Stiddard (2003) go on to question whether all such settings are able to be health promoting because this would require a philosophical shift in encouraging children to have a voice and have greater participation in developing their own learning agendas. This is an area that is receiving increasing attention (see Clark et al., 2005), and is explored later in this chapter when we consider the issue of listening to children in relation to promoting healthy eating.

In the later part of the twentieth century and the early twenty-first century, we can see that the focus has shifted away from health education to one of health promotion. Rather than the professional being viewed as expert on an individual's health, the focus is on people defining the health issues of importance to them. Crucially, rather than seeing health in terms of individual responsibility, there is a stress on collective, social responsibility for health. Thus, environmental and political action are features of health promotion approaches instead of health education approaches. Naidoo and Wills (2000) highlight how health promotion will probably involve a focus both on the individual, as in health education approaches, and on the structures that either support or impact negatively on people's health. In this sense, health promotion strategies embrace health education in part, but are broader in concern, involving greater state intervention.

In Chapter 4, we considered health inequalities in relation to food and eating. We saw how access to a healthy diet may be determined by a variety of factors, such as poverty. A focus on structural inequalities in relation to healthy eating might consider measures around ensuring *everyone* can afford a healthy diet as opposed to giving out food parcels or tokens to the most needy. Like the arguments for collectivist provision of school meals as compared to the residual school-meals service, the former focuses on provision for all rather than a targeted, potentially stigmatized service. The WHO (1986), for instance, argues that health and income are inextricably linked and any health promotion strategy should aim to challenge inequality.

Naidoo and Wills (2000) maintain that there are five main approaches to health promotion:

1   Medical or preventative

2   Behaviour change

3   Educational

4   Empowerment

5   Social change.

The *medical or preventative approach* tends to focus on prevention of diseases, but tends to be a top-down, expert-led approach to health. It is, however, very important in areas such as vaccination.

The *behaviour change approach* aims to encourage individuals to make changes to their lifestyles in order to improve their health. This approach tends to put the responsibility for making changes on to individuals rather than the structures that exist in society. It is also another example of a top-down approach to health, led by professionals.

The *educational approach* differs from the behaviour change approach because its aim is to provide people with information and knowledge, which will enable them to make informed choices about their lifestyle and associated health. The idea that individuals would want to make changes voluntarily to their lifestyles is an important concept that underpins this approach, and there is an assumption that increased knowledge will result in a change in behaviour.

Empowerment approaches, as we saw earlier in the chapter, focus on a reorientation of control, so individuals, as opposed to health professionals, have control of their own health and are enabled to make healthy choices in relation to their own lives. Naidoo and Wills (2000) note that this may include self-empowerment or community empowerment, the latter focusing on developing an approach where communities themselves act as advocates for change rather than relying on health professionals to do this for them. It therefore also involves a relinquishing of control by the health professional.

The final approach, *social change*, is sometimes referred to as 'radical health promotion' (Naidoo and Wills, 2000). This approach aims at challenging the structures which impact upon people's health, such as low income or racism. This approach is, arguably, more difficult for an individual practitioner to achieve as it may involve actively lobbying large government organizations. However, practitioners should consider how they can act as advocates of change, such as through working collaboratively with larger organizations or in groups.

Activity

Look at the following strategies to promote healthy eating and consider which approach they are most underpinned by:

▶ a food co-operative developed by a group of people in conjunction with a local organic food supplier to ensure a regular supply of locally grown, organic fruit and vegetables for the families taking part. The co-operative buys in bulk and cuts out the supermarket chain, thus making the food less expensive

▶ a health centre measuring children's body mass index in order to iden-tify children who are obese so as to target services to those families

▶ a practitioner, working with an obese child, encourages them to take exercise and make healthy food choices

▶ a large children's charity lobbying the government to ban the adver-tising of junk food on children's prime-time television

▶ a mass government campaign to persuade parents to give their chil-dren increased fruit and vegetables in their diet

▶ a nursery working with young children on a project about healthy eating in order to improve their knowledge, skills and attitudes in this area.

In thinking specifically about schools (and we would add early childhood set-tings to this), Beattie (2001: 137) argues that health promotion needs to work at a variety of levels and be multifaceted. He maintains that health promotion should operate at the levels of:

 ▶ curriculum content and pedagogy

 ▶ school ethos (such as staff–pupil relationships)

 ▶ environment (the physical space, facilities and support services)

 ▶ institution and structures (ultimately involving advocacy and campaigning).

What can be said about the different approaches to health promotion discussed so far is that they move from a position where the individual is the focus of attention, such as changing their dietary behaviour, to one where challenging structural inequalities is the focus of attention. This chapter now focuses specifically on the early years curriculum and how promoting healthy eating can be embedded within it.

Promoting healthy eating and the early years curriculum

In considering the early years curriculum, practitioners need to be thinking about everything the child encounters intentionally or unintentionally when they come to school or nursery. This would include specifically planned learning activities, possibly as part of a topic, if working with older children, as well as day-to-day routines, which, equally, require careful thinking through. Unintended learning relates to notions of the 'hidden curriculum' or the messages children receive from the school or nursery environment, which may or may not be the messages we hope they receive. Manning-Morton and Thorp (2003: 126) argue: 'Adopting a balanced approach means viewing the curriculum as more than a plan for play activities during non-routine times; it means giving appropriate time and thought to the whole day.'

Scriven and Stiddard (2003: 113) believe it is important to think of three key areas when considering health promotion as part of the curriculum:

1   Promoting a positive attitude

2   Building on knowledge

3   Increasing specific skills.

These three areas are embedded in the following discussion of meal-times, snacks and drinks, developing knowledge, skills and attitudes about food through play and structured activities, and planning for inclusion and equality. The new *Early Years Foundation Stage* (DfES, 2007) makes explicit reference to healthy eating as part of its self-care section under Personal, Social and Emotional Development as well as the health and bodily awareness section under Physical Development.

Activity

Search for the *Early Years Foundation Stage* on the website below and look for the references to food and eating.

www.standards.dfes/gov.uk/eyfs

Meal-times

Clearly, practitioners need to think carefully about ensuring children have access to a healthy diet during the day. This is especially important in full-day care settings, where young children may well have their breakfast, dinner and tea, as well as snacks (Moore et al., 2005). Alderton and Campbell-Barr's (2005) research suggests that the food and nutrition requirements of young children are often overlooked in early years settings and are considered only when there are cultural or medical reasons why a child might need variations in the food provided. They believe that training is crucial in order to improve practice as they identify a lack of nutritional knowledge amongst practitioners.

But it is not just what is eaten, but how it is eaten that is important. Practitioners need to ensure that they have time to focus on the child during meal-times rather than focusing on the task at hand because, as you will have noted from Chapter 5, meal-times offer an important time for developing relationships with young children. Whilst this closeness is often evident when feeding young babies, as they tend to be held during bottle-feeding, this closeness is not always evident with older children. When children are supported in a context of close relationships, they are able to show skills such as pouring their own drinks or feeding themselves at an early age (Petrie and Owen, 2005). In a school context, we have observed instances of young children being hurried through and having their food cut up for them when they are capable of cutting it up for themselves, because there is a focus on the task, that is, getting a large number of children through a hall quickly so another meal-time sitting can take place. Another practice to avoid is talking over children during meal-times rather than using the time to tune in to the child or small group of children. Careful consideration needs to be given to creating a calm and relaxed atmosphere to meal-times, such as allowing space for young children to sit in small groups rather than at a large, crowded table (Manning-Morton and Thorp, 2003) as this is more conducive to the tuning in to young children that we are advocating. Later in this chapter, we look at the issue of listening to young children more fully.

Cultural beliefs around how a child should eat are also important to acknowledge as Chapter 6 showed how food and eating are of key importance to one's sense of cultural identity. Whilst practitioners need to be aware of the cultural eating patterns of the children in their care, they also need to acknowledge their own beliefs in this area; beliefs that are likely to have been instilled from their own upbringing (Manning-Morton and Thorp, 2003). As Chapter 6 also noted, food and eating practices are key ways that children are inculcated into the particular culture they grow up in.

Reflection point

Look at the following examples of meal-time behaviours and reflect on which are similar to your own upbringing:

▸ eating at the table with your whole family – not when watching the television

▸ being told not to play with your food – it's dirty

▸ being told you have to eat everything on your plate before you can have a pudding

▸ being told you have to sit at the table until everyone has finished

▸ having to use a knife and fork as opposed to fingers when eating.

Now think about these in relation to your practice today. To what extent does your upbringing around appropriate meal-time behaviour impact upon your attitude to meal-time behaviours in your setting? Is there anything that challenges your sense of what is appropriate in the work that you do? Do you discuss your feelings around this with your team?

One of the most important ways that practitioners can develop a positive attitude towards healthy eating is during meal-times and snack-times, rather than one-off activities, because these are daily activities that form a crucial part of the rhythm of the day for young children (Albon, 2007; Viruru, 2001). Sepp et al. (2006) discuss how meal-times are important in developing table manners as well as food preferences. They discuss how in Sweden there has been a concept of a 'pedagogic meal' since the 1970s. 'The main point was that a role model seen every day by children was more powerful than verbal messages about a healthful diet and good table manners' (Sepp et al., 2006: 225).

Eating with the children is of key importance to the Swedish notion of the 'ped-agogic meal', as is the opportunity for children to observe what happens in kitchens day to day, such as how food is stored, prepared and cooked. This has meant ensuring that children are able to visit kitchens when they want to, rather than staff refusing the children visits on the basis of hygiene and safety. Despite this, Sepp et al.'s (2006) research found that early years practitioners did not see meal-times as a pedagogic activity, that is, an activity imbued with learning.

Reflection point

What do you view as the pedagogic activities in your setting? To what extent do you regard eating with the children as a pedagogic activity?

Snacks and drinks

Whilst it is crucial to address issues about meal-times, Cheater (2001) stresses the need to think of food, eating and drinking provision beyond this. Albon (2007) maintains that early years practitioners need to think carefully about whether to have a set snack-time or whether to have a self-service approach to snacks. She maintains that the former enables practitioners to ensure that all children have equal access to fruit and other snacks, but comes from a perspective where adults assume responsibility for children's hunger patterns. Alternatively, a self-service snack-time enables children to take responsibility for their own bodily needs but, in a large group situation, can make ensuring all children have equal access to food and drinks difficult, if not impossible, to achieve.

In settings that include children from birth to 3 as well as older children, practitioners need to think about how their philosophy in relation to food and eating is maintained through the age ranges, if indeed they think this is appro-priate. The babies may well be fed on demand and the youngest infants encour-aged to graze on healthy snacks whenever they wish to, whereas the older children may have to wait until set snack- and meal-times even if hungry, on the basis that they will have a 'healthy appetite' when it gets to such times (Lumeng, 2005). The former approach assumes that the child is expert on their own bodily needs and the latter suggests that adults should be in control of this or that the child's bodily needs are subservient to practical imperatives such as around lunch-time staff hours and even timetabling for the use of a space for meal-times.

Consideration of how drinks will be organized is another important consideration. Children need access to water throughout the day as dehydration can adversely affect their ability to learn (Haines et al., 2000). Sometimes the reason given for not having water readily available is because practitioners are concerned about the potential for spillages. The advent of water bottles, which, unlike cups, do not result in spillages, considerably lessens this issue.

Milk is important too because, apart from its benefits in relation to providing calcium and consequent bone development, it is **anti-cariogenic**, protecting teeth against decay. Cheese is particularly anti-cariogenic because it stimulates salivary flow and increases oral PH. Therefore, consumption of small amounts of cheese following a meal can reduce demineralization of tooth enamel (Moynihan, 2000). Practitioners might wish to think about this when menu-planning, whilst being aware of any lactose-intolerant children.

Developing knowledge, skills and attitudes about food through play and structured activities

The development of particular skills in relation to food and eating is also very important. This might include using a range of cultural implements in relation to eating, such as fingers, knives and forks, and chopsticks, but it might also refer to specific cookery skills. Burke (2002) argues that it is important that all children are taught cooking skills as well as developing an understanding of the ways in which nutrition relates to their short-term and long-term health. She reports that home economics in schools has developed into food technology, resulting in a lesser focus on cooking and nutrition and a greater emphasis on industrial and commercial concerns. Crucially, practical experience of food in terms of cooking is vital in improving children's healthy food choices (Burke, 2002). However it is not only cookery skills that need to be developed; Albon (2007) stresses the value of developing a curriculum *about* food as well as *through* food; arguing that it is often easier to concentrate on the latter rather than the former.

Promoting healthy eating is difficult as children come across many unhealthy messages about food, particularly in minority world societies at the present time. These might come through direct advertising of foods and messages children receive in popular culture such as children's television programmes. Despite this, Rivkin (2007) maintains that there are a range of strategies practitioners can adopt to develop a positive attitude to healthy eating:

- ▶ developing healthy cooking activities, such as making smoothies; fruit salads; dips and raw vegetables; soups; fruit kebabs and similar

- ▶ growing healthy foods in a garden area and using these in cookery activities

▸ visiting farmers' markets or similar on outings to explore seasonal, locally grown fruit and vegetables

▸ encouraging children to help with food preparation as they tend to enjoy foods they have played a part in preparing

▸ setting up a role-play area as a shop selling healthy produce, and trying to incorporate real foods into such play

▸ including a range of stories that are age-appropriate looking at topics such as food and nutrition.

Activity

Plan an activity for a group of children around a story about food. There are many useful stories and books in this area, such as:

Swain, G. (1999) *Eating*. London: Milet

Mills, D. and Brazell, D. (1999) *Lima's Red Hot Chilli*. London: Mantra

Try to make a collection of books, stories and rhymes in this area to act as a stimulus to activities and talking points around food and eating. Try to ensure that you develop a range of sources reflecting a range of cultural backgrounds – the book *Eating* by Gwenyth Swain, for instance, is useful in focusing on preparing, cooking, eating and sharing food in a variety of ways across cultures. It would also be interesting to make your own books in this area. As a practitioner, Debbie developed a variety of books and displays by lending a camera to parents and children, who took photographs at home of breakfast, lunch and tea as well as shopping, preparing and cooking food together. The photographs were shared and made into individual and collective books.

Practitioners may also want to think about whether they should offer pasta and other dried foods for collage or tactile play. From an ethical or 'green' perspective we might question whether food should be used as an art or play material, especially when there are people who have little or no food to eat in various parts of the world. There may be children in your setting who have experienced this and many children will be familiar with images of children living in such poverty. Conversely, playing with food may be useful in alleviating any anxieties a child might have in relation to food and eating, helping them to see food as an enjoyable part of life rather than something to feel stressed about. We may not stop a young child from playing with her food at meal-times when beginning to feed herself, so practitioners need to think carefully about the role of play in developing positive attitudes towards food and meal-times at other times of the day.

Adventures in Foodland (NHS Health Scotland, 2004), as the name suggests, stresses the importance of having fun with food. The pack of materials offers a range of ideas for food-use in play with very young children, as well as cooking ideas, and helps practitioners make links with the possible health benefits of such activities. As Martins (2006: 288) notes, learning about food is not just about learning what foods are 'good for you', it is also about 'developing a positive relationship with food'.

Reflection point

To what extent should food be used as a play material? What reasons do you give for your position?

Planning for inclusion and equality

McAuliffe and Lane (2005) argue that it is very important that practitioners introduce children to foods reflecting a range of cultures. However, we should note that for very young children, there may be security in having familiar foods. Whilst learning about unfamiliar foods can be a useful way to celebrate and learn about diversity, practitioners need to recognize that stereotypical assumptions are sometimes made about different groups of people and, as a consequence, less familiar foods may be seen as inferior. Because of this, there sometimes needs to be a process of unlearning of negative attitudes in order that a positive message gets across to the children.

McAuliffe and Lane (2005) suggest that practitioners need to ensure that they give equal value and respect to familiar and unfamiliar foods, including where and how the foods are produced, who produces them, and how they are eaten. They also argue that practitioners have an important role to play in being a positive role model in trying out unfamiliar foods and need to ensure they avoid language that reinforces cultural superiority. Examples to avoid that are given are 'ethnic foods' and 'normal foods'. The former ignores the fact that we all have ethnicity, so is incorrect, and the latter assumes what is normal is what the majority of children eat in a given place.

In planning for inclusion and equality, practitioners also need to think about gender in relation to food and eating. In an intriguingly titled study, *Burger Boy and Sporty Girl*, primary-school-aged children were shown a picture of burger, chips and coke and another picture of a more healthy meal option. The children were asked to describe the person who might eat these meals in some detail.

Ludvigsen and Sharma (2004) report how there was a strong gender divide evident in how the children viewed the possible consumers of these foods. They note,' Only very wealthy, clever, sporty girls could ever be imagined as choosing a healthy lunch – although nobody had ever met such a girl. *Real* boys definitely don't eat healthy food' (Ludvigsen and Sharma, 2004: 25).

Roos's (2002) study, which also looks at children's views, notes that children see the benefits of a healthy diet for girls in relation to appearance, that is, being thin and attractive, but for boys a healthy diet is seen in relation to being strong and active. However, the study also found that both girls and boys saw consumption of junk food and pizza as distinguishing children from adults.

The implication of studies such as these is that schools and early childhood settings need to be proactive in challenging such perceptions and need to think about the link between food and personal identity (as discussed in detail in Chapter 6 of this book). However, we need to recognize the difficulty of changing culturally embedded views around gender, identity, food and health.

Finally in this section, the needs of children with additional or special educational needs should be carefully thought through in relation to food and eating. The Council for Disabled Children (2004) advocate that parents and professionals caring for a disabled child should develop a communication passport which enables everyone to have the same information about how a child communicates and the passport may hold important information about a range of areas in the child's life including food and eating. They argue that it is important to tune into the perspectives of individual children. Examples given are that children with a disability, who find it difficult to feed themselves, may not want to wear a bib if older, but equally may not want to get dirty when feeding themselves. Therefore, a towel or old shirt may be a more suitable covering. Practitioners also need to be aware that some children may enjoy feeding themselves for a while, but find it tiring if for too long as well as frustrating if the food is getting cold.

In addition, children may feel differently about feeding themselves according to the food being eaten as well as the people they are eating with – especially if eating in a public space. Another consideration is that if a child needs their food mashed up before eating, practitioners should reflect on the opportunities the child has to experience the taste of individual foods as opposed to the taste of foods mashed up together. It may be difficult to understand what a child with a communication difficulty really likes and dislikes unless practitioners think carefully about their practice in this area.

Listening to children

In order to develop specific knowledge in relation to food and eating, early years practitioners need to build on children's own understandings of the food they eat. This involves tuning into children's perspectives. McAuliffe and Lane (2005: 1) maintain, 'Establishing links between food and learning supports the holistic philosophy of early years' practitioners. In addition, listening to young children is a core function of working with children and supporting their development and understanding. For young children, life isn't separated into education and care, or meal times and learning times – life is a seamless whole.'

An approach that listens to and values young children's points of view has its basis in a children's rights' perspective, as young children are seen as competent in being able to tell us about their needs, and as having a unique knowledge about their own lives as lived by them now (Kjorholt, 2005; Underdown, 2007). Importantly, listening should be part of an approach which involves tuning in to children as individuals and be about their everyday lives (McAuliffe and Lane, 2005). This tuning-in process may involve creative approaches to the notion of 'listening' as the idea that children are only speaking to us when verbal, is limiting, both to very young children and to children who have communication difficulties, and indeed to some adults.

Close observation is a key tool for early years practitioners in helping them to tune in to children – particularly very young children and babies (Manning-Morton and Thorp, 2003). Observation of the particular facial expressions, movements of head and tongue, and the vocalizations a child makes, for instance, may all be cues to the practitioner about the child's feelings about a particular food or meal-time experience. As noted in Chapter 5, when practitioners work in a way where they act as a key person to a small group of children (Elfer et al., 2003), an understanding of such idiosyncratic cues is likely to be heightened significantly owing to the close relationship between child and practitioner. Therefore, it is vital that a child's key person is the person who supports them at meal-times for as much of the time as is possible.

An approach to working with children that incorporates their perspectives on the food they eat is discussed by McAuliffe and Lane (2005). They describe how one setting incorporated children's perspectives into their menu-planning. Strategies used included:

- ▶ running tasting sessions with the children
- ▶ establishing a café as a role-play area, with staff engaging children in discussion around likes and dislikes around food as well as keeping observational notes about the children's play
- ▶ working with the cook with evidence gathered to produce menus that are both responsive to young children's preferences and nutritionally balanced.

Involving parents in promoting healthy eating

Cashden (1998) argues that the first three years of life are crucial in establishing good eating patterns. Given that parents are usually young children's primary carers, this suggests that practitioners need to work with parents from a very early stage in promoting healthy eating.

The evidence, however, is mixed regarding parental influence. Piperakis et al. (2004) argue that school-based nutrition programmes should involve parents because they are more influential than schools in determining lasting good dietary habits. Conversely, Lumeng (2005) argues that in the face of the obesogenic environment we live in, parents' influence is limited because there are societal and biological influences that limit the control a parent might have over their child's eating behaviour. One such societal influence might be the advertising of junk food to children during children's prime-time television. Whatever one's perspective, early years practitioners need to think carefully about what they mean by working in partnership with parents in relation to promoting healthy eating.

Partnership with parents

Partnership working with parents is important because both early years practitioners and parents have knowledge that can be shared for the benefit of children. Pinkerton (2001: 251) argues, 'At the core of partnership lies a purposeful relationship in which two or more parties engage because they share a goal and recognise that it is only through pooling their resources and agreeing on how best to work together that the goal can be met'.

Braun (1992) notes the importance of practitioners avoiding making assumptions about individual parents or neighbourhoods and advocates that the foundations of partnership working lie in a clear recognition of the different skills and experiences parents and practitioners bring to the task of promoting the welfare of the child. In the following case study, try to think about whether the health visitor's approach could be described as partnership working.

Case study

Julie lives in a small flat in a large block of flats that she rents from a housing association on the edge of a large city. She has two children, Jamie, aged 2 years and Tom, aged 3 years. Julie is a lone parent, who

(Continued)

(Continued)

works part time as a cleaner. One of the health visitors in the area is running a series of classes called 'How to Give your Child A Healthy Lunch-Box' and has put posters around the estate Julie lives on to publicize these. To Julie's knowledge no one in the local community has asked for these classes to be run and few people know the health visitor as she is new to the team.

Julie finds the health visitor's approach highly patronizing, saying, 'It's like she (the health visitor) doesn't think we know what's good for our children. I think I do OK, especially as it's a long walk to the nearest supermarket. I know it's better for my kids to eat fruit and to put things like watercress and salad stuff in their sandwiches with the ham or cheese, but my kids don't like it – they just pull it out and complain. My two kids would eat pineapple and expensive fruits if I could afford them but don't like things like apples and oranges. I don't earn enough money to have my kids not eat something I give them, so I give them foods I know they'll eat. They (health visitors) don't run classes in their own communities but assume that just because we live on an estate like this we need to have lessons in how to feed our kids. Give me some extra money and I'd give my kids lots of fruit and stuff.'

Using the approaches to health promotion outlined earlier in the chapter, reflect upon the approach of the health visitor and consider whether the issue is one of needing to change the behaviour of individuals or to try to tackle inequality, such as the proximity of a supermarket selling affordable fruit and vegetables, and low income.

Practitioners can work in partnership with parents and carers in a number of ways: in relation to improving nursery menus, Stanner (2004) maintains:

▶ parents need to be involved in any changes in food provisioning rather than having changes sprung upon them

▶ parents need to know what is on the nursery menu a week in advance in order to plan their own food provisioning accordingly

▶ settings should give clear information to parents about *what* their child has eaten and the *amount* eaten during the day

▸ settings should ensure they have up-to-date information about any dietary needs of the children; parents are often able to give detailed information about allergies and special dietary requirements, for instance

▸ recipes for dishes that are both healthy *and* popular with the children should be shared between parents and settings.

Lumeng (2005: 18) believes that there are four things practitioners should do in working with parents in the area of promoting healthy eating:

▸ acknowledge the limits of parental influence (we would also add the practitioner's influence)

▸ empower parents to advocate changes to meal-times in early childhood settings. This may be around the food itself or the meal-time experience

▸ refrain from encouraging parents to change their feeding practices when there is little research evidence to support this. Professionals must recognize the myriad of feeding practices and their sociocultural bases

▸ act as an advocate. Professionals should act as advocates for change at a policy level, such as campaigning for an increase in the availability of affordable, healthy foods for families on low incomes. This is essential in preventing childhood obesity.

Sellers et al. (2005: 240) conclude, 'Providers and parents can join forces with others in the community to become advocates for children and argue for healthier communities that are supportive of healthy diets and active lifestyles'. In other words, by working in partnership with parents and carers, early childhood practitioners can have a positive impact on the health of young children.

Developing a health promotion programme

Sometimes it is appropriate for early years settings to organize a specific health promotion programme around healthy eating. This may be as a result of a local or national initiative, or as part of delivering this aspect of the Early Years Foundation Stage curriculum. Whatever the reasons behind the initiative, there are several steps to take when planning a health promotion programme (Mukherji, 2005):

▸ identification of needs and priorities

▸ setting aims and objectives

▸ deciding on the best way to achieve these aims

▸ identification of resource needs and available resources

▸ action plan

▸ implementation

▸ evaluation.

Identification of needs and priorities

This will relate to the specific needs of the setting, for instance you may have concerns about the quality of children's packed lunches, or you may have several children who are overweight in the setting. It is at this stage that you need to involve all interested parties, including parents and outside agencies.

Setting aims and objectives

Clear aims and objectives need to be identified and incorporated in your short-, medium- and long-term planning. You may decide that one of your aims is to redesign the setting's menus and to instigate healthy snacks instead of sweets and crisps. An aim that involves parents may be to encourage parents to provide healthy lunch-boxes. Any planning you do for children-centred activities should also link into the Early Years Foundation Stage curriculum (Mukherji, 2005).

Deciding on the best ways to achieve your aims

Depending upon your specific aims you should identify people who can help, and it is at this stage that you will be thinking about the most effective way of introducing the topic to the children.

Identifying resource needs and available resources

Once you know what you want to do and more or less how you are going to go about it, you need to seek out resources to help you. Resources may include funding, expertise, parental help as well as books, posters, and so on.

Action plan

An action plan clearly indicating what needs to be done, by whom and by when will be very useful. Someone should have the responsibility for monitoring the plan to see if the various tasks have been achieved.

Implementation

This is the phase of the programme when the results of your planning come together. The person monitoring the action plan should review if all is going smoothly, and make changes to the programme if needed.

Evaluation

Built into the action plan should be some sort of evaluation measure(s) related to the aims/objectives of the campaign. For instance, if you want to improve the quality of packed lunches you need to have an objective measure of what was in packed lunches to start with. The staff team should have a debriefing session where they can discuss the things that went well, and the things that could be improved upon. Observations of the children's involvement/understanding should be shared to identify opportunities for further activities. Someone should have the responsibility of archiving all the records of the programme, so that in future years, if a similar campaign is to be planned, there are resources available. Keeping electronic copies of letters, planning and so on will make things much easier the next time around. Finally, all those who helped should be formally thanked.

Summary

▶ There is a range of approaches to health promotion that underpin the strategies early years practitioners use to promote healthy eating in their settings (and, indeed, beyond them). These range from approaches that focus on changing individual behaviour to approaches that focus on empowerment and social change.

▶ Food and eating is a crucial part of early childhood practice and needs careful consideration. Practitioners need to consider meal-time routines as well as the provision of snacks and drinks. They also need to think about how they develop a positive attitude towards food and eating alongside developing children's nutritional understanding.

▶ Practitioners need to plan carefully to ensure that issues of equality and inclusion are addressed. The experience of food and eating is coloured by race and ethnicity, gender, age and ability.

▶ Listening to, and building on, children's perspectives around food and eating is important as it is an area of fundamental importance to human lives.

▶ Working in *partnership* with parents is vital in any strategy for promoting healthy eating in young children.

▶ Practitioners can actively involve themselves in health promotion by planning a health promotion campaign.

Discussion points

▶ Reflect on the degree to which you try to tune in to children's perspectives regarding meal-times and snack-times. What strategies do you use to tune in to the perspectives of children with special educational needs?

▶ Do you operate a set snack time or a self-service approach to snacks? Reflect on the reasoning behind your practice.

▶ How can you improve the ways in which you work with parents to promote healthy eating in and beyond your setting?

Further reading

Naidoo, J. and Wills, J. (2000) *Health Promotion: Foundations for Practice*. 2nd ed. Edinburgh: Bailliere Tindall.

NHS Health Scotland (2004) *Adventures in Foodland: Ideas for Making Food Fun from an Early Age*. Edinburgh: Health Scotland.

Sellers, K., Russo, T.J., Baker, I. and Dennison, B.A. (2005) 'The role of childcare providers in the prevention of childhood overweight', *Journal of Early Childhood Research*, 3(3): 227–42.

Useful web sites

www.healthyschools.gov.uk/ This is the Healthy Schools web site (superseded 'Wired for Health')

www.healthpromotingschools.co.uk/

(Accessed on 25 July 2007)

Multidisciplinary Working

This final chapter examines multidisciplinary working in relation to children, food and eating. The area is important because increasingly, professionals are being asked to work together to promote children's health – our concern here being healthy eating. The chapter considers the different roles professionals have in relation to developing healthy eating and preventing obesity, and stresses the importance of the early childhood practitioner in this area. In addition, the chapter highlights the importance of multidisciplinary perspectives in the study of food and eating as each perspective brings a different understanding of the issue.

This concluding chapter examines a key area of early childhood practice; multidisciplinary working. The focus of the chapter is in looking at the roles different professionals play in relation to young children's dietary intake and the range of academic disciplines that contribute to our understanding of the food and eating practices of young children and their families. In particular, the chapter makes the case for boundary or border crossing to denote the way professionals can learn from working collaboratively with a range of partners as well as in the field of research; working across disciplines to develop a richer understanding of the complexity of food and health in early childhood.

The chapter looks at the following key areas:

▸ Why is multidisciplinary working important in the area of children's food and eating?

▸ What do we mean by multidisciplinary working?

▸ Benefits and barriers to multidisciplinary working

▸ Researching children's food and eating – the importance of multidisciplinary working

Why is multidisciplinary working important in the area of children's food and eating?

There has been a range of policy initiatives in recent years that promote the idea of multidisciplinary or multi-agency working. Many of these are in the areas of safeguarding and working with children with special educational needs – to name but two – such as the Common Assessment Framework and the Lead Professional (see www.everychildmatters for information about these). The Every Child Matters agenda (DfES, 2003) focuses all professionals on working towards five outcomes, which will enable *all* children to have the support they need to:

- be healthy

- stay safe

- enjoy and achieve

- make a positive contribution

- achieve economic well-being.

Throughout the Every Child Matters agenda there is a stated need for professionals to work together, which might involve co-locating some health services into children's centres, for instance. In relation to obesity, the focus is on prevention and early intervention rather than dealing with the consequences of being obese. As with other aspects of health promotion, tackling childhood obesity is a complex task. At one level it can be seen as an individual task with parents being given the responsibility to monitor the weight of their own children. However, because the causes of childhood obesity are multifactorial, interventions need to be targeted at community and government levels as well as at the individual child.

In order to promote a cross-governmental approach, a public service agreement (PSA) was set up between the departments of Health, Education and Skills and Culture, Media and Sport 'to halt, by 2010, the year-on-year increase in obesity among children under 11 in the context of a broader strategy to tackle obesity in the population as a whole' (DoH, 2004b: 13). Unfortunately no funds were specifically set aside for this, and no specific programmes were set up to tackle child obesity. The approach taken was to impact upon health promotion programmes that are designed to have a positive effect upon the diet and lifestyle of children. There are four main programmes: School-Meals, the School Sport Strategy, the Healthy Schools Programme and the Children's Play Initiative (HCPAC, 2007).

In its 2007 report, the HCPAC notes that since the public service agreement was set up there have been no more up-to-date figures for childhood obesity produced, so it is not possible to make a judgement as to the effectiveness of the

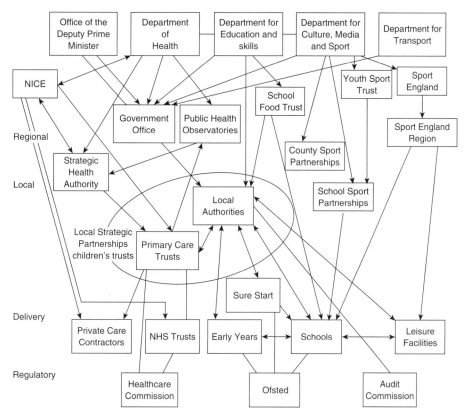

Figure 8.1 The delivery chain for tackling childhood obesity.

Source: The House of Commons Public Accounts Committee (2007: 8)

various interventions. However they do point out the number of different organizations involved and the complexity of co-ordinating these initiatives, as demonstrated by the diagrammatic representation in Figure 8.1.

Reflection point

Is your setting or workplace involved in any initiatives to prevent childhood obesity? Have these initiatives been generated by you or your team, or are they part of a wider scheme? What do you consider your role to be in the prevention of childhood obesity?

Another example of a cross-departmental initiative can be seen in the White Paper *Choosing Health* (DoH, 2004c). As part of the Choosing Health agenda

(DoH, 2004c), a national delivery plan focusing on nutrition and activity is due to be published, which will co-ordinate with the government Strategy on Sustainable Farming and Food. In other words, government departments are also working together on developing a more sustainable approach to food production and consumption. As well as this, the Public Sector Food Procurement Initiative, launched in 2003, is another example of an initiative that aims to ensure government departments work together to procure foods that promote sustainable development. An example would be supporting schools in tendering for foods from smaller, local suppliers (www.foodinschools). These initiatives are further examples of the way that green issues are linked increasingly to the health agenda with working together across government departments and with business, an expression of the way the government sees this being delivered.

At a local level, there are a number of professional groups that play an important role in improving children's diets. Robinson (2006) outlines some case studies that illustrate their respective roles. Some of these are described below.

Community dietician

Community dieticians work to meet local and national health targets regarding lowering the incidence of diabetes, obesity and heart disease (to name but a few). In addition to this, they work with individuals as part of the work of health centres and community hospitals. They might specialize in supporting people who cannot manage an oral diet owing to illness or disability. Where possible the community dietician will get involved in health promotion work. However, in some areas, their work may be primarily clinical in focus, such as working with individuals around devising and maintaining an appropriate diet plan through consultation, as well as monitoring through attendance at clinics. Community dieticians are usually based in local primary care trusts (PCTs) in localities or as part of the community dietetics service in local acute hospital trusts.

Dental health promotion team

Community dentists are usually dentists who have undertaken additional training in meeting the needs of people who have phobias about dentistry or who have additional needs. A senior dental officer is likely to have undertaken postgraduate study in health promotion. This person is likely to spend some time engaged in clinical work and some time in health promotion – for instance, they might facilitate the practice of other workers such as dental therapists, who visit playgroups and nurseries. They might work with schools on promoting dental health as part of the community dental service and help to produce dental health resources as well as deliver training in this area.

School nurse

School nurses are registered general nurses or children's nurses who have obtained community experience. There is also a specialist qualification in school nursing. The school nursing service is a service that is open to all families and other agencies. School nurses work with a range of professionals such as social services and Sure Start programmes. As part of their work they might work with a Healthy Schools team to develop its healthy eating policy, or work with a child (and family) who is overweight or who has poor dental health, and with many other aspects of health-related work in schools. All schools have access to the school nursing service and children can be referred in a variety of ways, such as through their GP, their parents or their school. Service level agreements outline the particular work a school nurse will engage in with a particular school.

As well as the professionals outlined in Robinson (2006), we also need to consider the early years practitioner.

Early years practitioner

In thinking about the professionals that have a role to play in promoting healthy eating in early childhood and beyond, it is important not to neglect the vital role played by the early years practitioner (Albon, 2006), which might include nursery nurses, early years teachers, early years professionals and teaching assistants. Early years practitioners are particularly well placed to play a key role in developing healthy eating because of a number of significant features of their work:

▸ They will often see children more regularly and for longer periods than any other group of professionals – often daily.

▸ Their work is often directed towards the care of the young child in a way unlike that of other professionals, such as providing meals, snacks and drinks, thus making a significant contribution to the actual diet imbibed by the children.

▸ They will often be involved in helping children to make healthy choices by improving their knowledge of how a healthy diet can contribute to a healthy lifestyle.

▸ They will often be involved in helping children to develop self-care skills such as feeding themselves in a way unlike other professionals.

▸ They will often see parents and carers more regularly than any other group of professionals.

Activity

Make a list of key professionals not included in the list above who play an important role in ensuring children and their families have a healthy diet. In doing this, research the particular role these professionals play in relation to promoting healthy eating. Review your own practice – how much contact do you have with these professionals?

Each of the professional groups above have a role to play in promoting healthy eating and preventing obesity. However, whilst we might use the term 'multidisciplinary' to denote the ways in which professionals might work together, there are variations in the way such terminology is used.

What do we mean by multidisciplinary working?

In this chapter we have been using the term 'multidisciplinary' very broadly to denote a range of ways that different professionals or researchers might work together. This section examines some examples of working together in practice as well as terminology relating to practice that might come under the turn of phrase 'multidisciplinary' that we employ. What needs to be stressed is the wide variety of ways that people use terminology in this area, and the need for people to be clear how such terms are being used in a particular context.

Anning et al. (2006: 27), drawing on the work of Ovreveit, maintain that there are a number of ways that different professional groups work together. These might include:

- a team of professionals who are line managed by the same person – at a very simple level, this might be teachers, special needs' assistants and nursery nurses working together in a nursery class under the leadership of a primary school headteacher

- a 'core and extended team', where the core team are managed by the same leader but there are extended team members who are line-managed by an external agency – an example of this might be a children's centre where the core team include family support workers with a social work background as well as teachers and nursery nurses (early years practitioners). The extended team might include professionals managed by the local primary care trust, such as community dieticians, speech and language therapists, educational psychologists, community midwives and health visitors

▸ a 'network association', where different professionals do not work together formally but work with the same client or group of clients and meet together to share practice around this. An example of this might be a social worker, community dietician, health visitor and early years practitioner working together with a family who have an obese child.

Naidoo and Wills (2000) unpick the different terms that are used to describe the ways that professionals work together in relation to health promotion. They distinguish these relationships as:

▸ *Partnership* – here there is sharing of power and joint action between agencies at local and national level.

▸ *Service agreements and contracts* – these are set out to make clear the mutual responsibilities each partner has in relation to improving health.

▸ *Multiagency* – this refers to organizations belonging to the same sector such as health, education or social services, that is, for Naidoo and Wills, groups working together from the *statutory* providers of public services.

▸ *Intersectoral* – this differs from multiagency working because more than one sector might be involved, such as the public sector, private sector and voluntary groups. Naidoo and Wills note that the World Health Organization uses the term 'intersectoral collaboration' to describe the process whereby different partners such as health authorities, business, voluntary bodies, government and individuals work together to improve health.

▸ *Inter-disciplinary or multidisciplinary working* – this might include the joint working of people with different roles within the same organization or across sectors. You will note that this is narrower than our own usage of the term.

▸ *Joint planning* – this is where organizations develop and implement a joint plan from jointly agreed objectives developed within or across sectors.

▸ *Teams* – these may be multidisciplinary, defined as a team developed from the same organization, or be multiagency, for instance. The key characteristic, for Naidoo and Wills, is the sharing of a common task and the composition of the team, consisting of professionals chosen for their particular knowledge and expertise. (This list is summarized from Naidoo and Wills, 2000: 157–8.)

Case study

Farshad is 4 years old and is considered obese. He attends a nursery class attached to a primary school mornings only. He can barely stand up unaided from sitting on the floor and finds it difficult to take part in vigorous physical exercise outdoors, such as playing football, as this makes him breathless. Children in the nursery notice that he looks different and the staff have noticed that they are beginning to call him names and make negative comments about his weight. The staff are becoming increasingly concerned about Farshad's weight and the effect it is having on his general health.

The early years practitioners in the nursery class have carried out activities around healthy eating with the children and each child has a piece of fruit at snack time. However they have noticed that Farshad's mother – Amina – brings him a sugary drink each day and greets him with chocolate and crisps at home time. They have spoken to Amina informally about this, but to no effect. In addition, the early years practitioners have carried out a series of healthy eating workshops for parents, but have been unable to encourage Amina to attend; attendance has been primarily from parents the practitioners perceive to have taken on board the 'healthy eating message'. As yet, the practitioners have not contacted any other professional groups regarding this family.

Amina says that she likes to ensure Farshad has a meal he enjoys and cannot afford for him to waste any food. She rarely takes him to the local playground because it is vandalized and in a poor state and she feels uncomfortable because the playground is used primarily by white families who have made racist comments towards her. She and Farshad rarely go out and have few friends or family in the area and Amina confides that sharing sweets and crisps whilst watching videos is something they really enjoy together.

This case study highlights the complexity of working with families who have an obese child. In reflecting on the issues presented here, consider which professional groups might need to become involved with a family such as this, and why, and the particular roles they might bring to this. Imagine, too, that this is a family in the setting you work in. Using the earlier discussion in this section, how would you characterize the way you would work with other professionals and partner agencies in this instance?

(Continued)

Finally, think about the issue of partnership with parents, discussed in the previous chapter, and reflect on how Amina might feel having a potentially large group of professionals working with her to improve Farshad's diet and exercise, and consequently his health. In doing this, think back to some of the issues discussed in Chapter 6 around gender, identity and food; for many women, feeding their children is more than just ensuring they receive their required nutrients for the day – it is an activity permeated with strong emotions, not least the pleasure a woman might get from seeing her family enjoy eating the food she has provided for them. Lupton (1996: 42) observes that an infant's body is symbolic of the 'mother's ability to feed and care for it well' and as such is subject to a high degree of surveillance from professionals, other parents and the media – to name but a few. Consider how professionals might be sensitive to this alongside keeping the welfare of the child uppermost in their minds.

It would seem that there are a range of ways that professionals might work collaboratively and the case study above encourages you to consider how this might possibly be experienced by the parent, Amina. Despite the shifts in government policy towards promoting different forms of co-operation between professionals, agencies and sectors, there are potentially significant barriers to multidisciplinary working. The next section looks at the benefits and barriers that might be experienced when working in this way.

Benefits and barriers to multidisciplinary working

Naidoo and Wills (2000: 162) maintain that there are many advantages to working together in health promotion:

▸ By bringing together a wide range of people, some of whom would not see themselves as health professionals, a more holistic approach to health promotion is fostered as opposed to a treatment–centred approach to health. As this chapter has noted, early years practitioners should see themselves as having a crucial role to play in promoting healthy eating – possibly this is a role that teachers, in particular, have not always seen as part of their professional practice.

▸ Through working together, organizations develop greater understanding of each other's roles, which can help to negate rivalries. An example of such rivalry might be a health visitor feeling that an early years practitioner should not be running a parent workshop on healthy eating

▸ The public are less likely to receive conflicting messages, such as around what is a healthy diet during pregnancy.

▸ There is likely to be a more comprehensive understanding of local needs because the diverse roles of professionals give them different insights into local issues – one might compare the knowledge a reception teacher in a local school might have in relation to that of a community midwife.

▸ It is helpful in ensuring that there is a more accurate targeting of services as well as identification of gaps in service provision.

▸ Administrative costs can be minimized through joint commissioning of services.

▸ Broader issues relating to ill health may be dealt with owing to the wider level of expertise drawn upon. An example of this might be the private, voluntary and statutory sectors working together to address the availability of fresh fruit and vegetables in an area, thus addressing the wider issue of health inequality.

Wright (2001) outlines the many health initiatives that have been developed in the past 10 years that have provided opportunities for professionals to work together in innovative ways to improve the health of local populations. These include the development of Health Improvement Programmes, Health Action Zones and Healthy Living Centres. Wright is positive about the benefits to the health of populations of such collaborative working but recognizes that this involves 'crossing organisational, professional and cultural boundaries' (Wright, 2001: 52). Such boundary-crossing can be problematic. Albon (2007) notes that there can be unwillingness to think beyond one's own professional training, particularly in a context of an ever-increasing range of government and local initiatives that have been developed around healthy eating and the time that these take to implement and sustain. For Markwell and Speller (2001), there is acknowledgement that working across professional boundaries can be especially difficult during times of change, conflict and organizational development.

But boundary-crossing may offer a more fundamental challenge; a challenge to one's sense of professional identity. Molyneux (2001: 33) draws upon the work of Laidler, in particular her notion of 'professional adulthood'. The idea of 'professional adulthood' is developed from a notion of staff from a range of professional backgrounds feeling confident and secure enough in their own professional identities to move to a position where they can work effectively with staff from other professional backgrounds. Whilst ideas and expertise are shared across multi-professional teams, what underpins this is the importance of professionals holding on to the expertise of their own professional background. In other words, one needs to be secure within one's own professional identity in order to develop successful relationships with people from other professional backgrounds. Anning et al. (2006) also believe that multi-professional working can challenge one's sense of professional identity. They maintain that, 'As child welfare policy shifts towards integration and joined-up thinking, professionals will face profound shifts and challenges in terms of their sense of personal identity' (Anning et al., 2006: 61).

Molyneux (2001: 34) particularly focuses on the issue of power, and argues that,

> Health care professionals need to reflect on, and reconsider their attitudes, approaches and expectations towards both traditional ways of working and professional power balances in interprofessional settings ... Encouragement and opportunity needs to be provided from management to staff working in such settings, enabling them to develop creative methods of working, most suited to their own particular setting and service user group.

Whilst Molyneux is talking about inter-professional working, which she defines as relating to where a range of professionals work closely as part of a single team, much of what she says is applicable to early years practitioners who work with a range of professionals, albeit in a range of different partnership contexts. Her discussion of balances of power between different professionals has important resonance for early childhood practice.

There has been a tendency to elevate practice pertaining to education over the care of young children. This has resulted in some professionals and the knowledge and skills they possess being given greater credence than others – notably, in relation to early years practitioners; teachers over nursery nurses. Manning-Morton (2006) notes that a view of professionalism has emerged that elevates knowledge of children's *learning* over the skills involved in *caring* for young children. Albon (2007) argues that this asymmetry of status has its basis in long-standing debates about mind-body duality and the perceived importance of controlling the body in order to develop the mind (see also Manning-Morton, 2006, who adds the lesser importance often placed on the emotions). A key concern for Manning-Morton (2006) is that practitioners – her concern being under 3 practitioners – develop self-awareness; indeed her article includes the phrase 'The Personal is Professional ...' to encapsulate the view that professional and personal identity are entwined. This is also of primary interest to Elliot (2007). In other words, it is not just professional identity but personal identity that is important here. Our inclusion of reflection points to encourage you to think about both your own personal attitudes and your professional practice, is an expression of the importance we place on this.

Anning et al. (2006) note that professionals regarded as having a lower status are often not asked to discuss the work they do with others. Arguably, this mirrors Lupton's (1996) discussion of the invisibility of caring work around food and eating, which is carried out primarily by women in the private sphere of the home. This invisibility of care is also replicated in early childhood practice as there is a vast array of care activities relating to food and eating that are rarely acknowledged. These might include:

▸ working with parents to support them with weaning their baby

▸ supporting children with washing their hands before meal-times and cooking activities; promoting good hygiene around food

▸ eating one's lunch alongside young children and the possible challenge this might present in terms of personal feelings around children playing with food and making a mess

▸ organizing the nursery environment in a way conducive to a happy, relaxed, supportive meal-time experience for all children

▸ supporting children to prepare their own snacks, such as washing or peeling fruit

▸ working with parents to ensure children's transition to having meals at the nursery is a smooth one

▸ ensuring that scrupulous food storage and preparation standards are adhered to, including the preparation of babies' bottles

▸ encouraging a reluctant eater to try something on their plate

▸ supporting children to feed themselves with increasing independence

▸ supporting a child with communication difficulties to make choices about the food he or she eats

▸ preparing an attractively presented and nutritious tea for a group of children.

Reflection point

Review your own practice in relation to the number of care activities that relate to food and eating in your setting. We are sure that you will be able to add many other activities to this list. In doing this, consider the amount of time that is taken up with planning and discussing such activities and compare this with the time you spend planning for play activities that are not part of everyday routines – sometimes one-off experiences!

(Continued)

If you are a manager, consider how you support practitioners to enable them to give such care activities a high priority. Are rotas organized so that practitioners can support their key children at meal-times for the majority of the time? What happens if practitioners are on holiday or off sick? Do you encourage team members to share their feelings, knowledge and skills about this aspect of care on a regular basis? Do you, yourself, give this high priority?

Anning et al. (2006) argue that whilst multi-professional teams offer an opportunity for professionals to share their practice in a wide range of areas, colleagues from different disciplines may well challenge some of the underlying assumptions behind the work that they do in an attempt to get to know more about the work of their professional colleagues. This may well be a challenging experience. A secure professional identity, as noted earlier in this section, and a willingness to be self-reflexive (Manning-Morton, 2006) is an important prerequisite to this.

Activity

Try to share an aspect of your meal or snack-time practice with someone from a different professional background. Ask them for their perspectives on what you do – you might even like to try and invite them in to observe what you do at first hand. In doing this, try to be open to different perspectives of your practice.

Researching children's food and eating – the importance of multidisciplinary working

Whilst it is important for practitioners to embrace multidisciplinary working, it is also important in the area of academic study and research. Muñoz and Jeris (2005: 5) maintain that 'through exposure and collaboration clinicians learn in what ways their discipline overlaps with others, and the role of others in service delivery'. They argue that as professions have become increasingly specialized, they have lost a sense of their interrelatedness, especially in universities where they compete for scarce resources. Inter-professional training and education may be important owing to the opportunity it gives for collaborative working and developing relationships across professional disciplines (Wright, 2001).

Dahlberg and Moss (2005) utilize the term 'border crossing' to refer to the exploration of writers and traditions from a range of disciplines, some of which may not write specifically about early childhood but whose theoretical insights help shed new light on the subject. Food and eating, we would argue, is an area that offers exciting opportunities for multidisciplinary working and research.

In writing this book we have drawn upon research from a range of academic disciplines:

- ‣ nutritional science
- ‣ health studies
- ‣ social anthropology
- ‣ sociology
- ‣ psychology
- ‣ cultural studies
- ‣ social policy
- ‣ physiology.

These are but a few of the disciplines that might be employed in the study of children, food and eating. By drawing on a range of disciplines, we are encouraged to look at children's diet and dietary behaviour through new lenses (Albon, 2005). Richardson (2000), when discussing writing up research, uses the metaphor of a crystal to think about the way light changes; reflecting and refracting according to the position through which we look through the lens. She states that she employs the image of a crystal because it

> combines symmetry and substance with an infinite variety of shapes, substances, transmutations, multidimensionalities, and angles of approach ... Crystals are prisms that reflect externalities and refract within themselves, creating different colours, patterns and arrays, casting off in different directions. What we see depends on our angle of repose. (Richardson, 2000: 934)

This is a metaphor we would like to apply to the study of food and eating. Thus, by looking at children's food and eating through the lens of psychoanalytical theory we might focus in detail on areas such as a baby's experience of breast-feeding in the context of their close emotional attachment to their mother; conversely, the lens of social anthropology encourages us to focus on the wider sociocultural context in which food and eating occurs. Each discipline has an important role to play in further developing our understanding of children's food and eating (Albon, 2005). Furthermore, within each discipline, professionals, parents and children will each add their own particular insights that contribute to a richer understanding of the subject. The challenge for multidisciplinary working is in changing 'our angle of repose', as Richardson (2000) puts it, in order to gain alternative, fresh insights into practice.

In writing this book, we have employed a range of perspectives that we feel are important in the area of food and health in early childhood. There are many others that we have not had room to include. However, we hope that we have encouraged you to draw upon a range of disciplines to extend your understanding of food and eating further and, consequently, to enrich your practice. Food and eating are of fundamental importance to human lives and are therefore of fundamental importance for early childhood practice.

Summary

▸   There are a range of local and national initiatives that focus on the need for different professionals to work together in order to improve children's diets as well as tackle obesity.

▸   There are a range of professionals who have different roles in relation to children's food and eating and it is important to continue to develop an understanding of these roles.

▸   Early years practitioners are particularly well placed to promote healthy eating in early childhood, primarily because they see children on a regular, often daily, basis.

▸   There is a range of terminology and working practices that come under the umbrella 'multidisciplinary' and we need to be sure what terms mean in particular contexts.

▸   There are many benefits as well as barriers to multidisciplinary working. A key barrier may be philosophical, relating to the elevation of education and knowledge over the skill of caring for young children. This has resulted in a higher status of some professionals over others.

▸   Multidisciplinary working applies to study and research as well as practice as it encourages us to view the issue of food and eating from different perspectives and thus enriching our practice.

Discussion points

▸   Did your professional training prepare you for developing a healthy eating programme in your setting? If not, what key knowledge and skills do you feel you need to develop?

▸ What are your biggest personal and professional challenges in relation to multidisciplinary working?

▸ Which perspectives on food and eating are you most drawn towards – psychological, as in Chapter 5, sociological, as in Chapter 6 or from nutritional science, as in Chapter 2 (or any of the many other perspectives we have drawn upon)? When considering this, think about the personal and professional experiences you have had and how they may have impacted on this.

Further reading

Albon, D. (2005) 'Approaches to the study of children, food and sweet-eating: a review of the literature', *Early Child Development and Care*, 175(5): 407–417.

Anning, A., Cottrell, D. Frost, N., Green, J. and Robinson, M. (2006) *Developing Multiprofessional Teamwork for Integrated Children's Services*. Maidenhead: Open University Press.

Manning-Morton, J. (2006) 'The personal is professional: professionalism and the birth to threes practitioner', *Contemporary Issues in Early Childhood*, 7(1): 42–52.

Useful web sites

http://www.foodvision.gov.uk/

http://www.everychildmatters.gov.uk/

(Accessed 25 July 2007)

Glossary

Absolute poverty. A family is said to live in absolute poverty if family income is insufficient to meet the basic needs of life, such as food, shelter and clothing (Townsend, 1979).

Adipose tissue. A collection of cells storing fat.

Agency. Whilst you may be familiar with the term 'agency' in relation to an organization you work for, in this instance, the term, is used to denote the way that children are not passive recipients of food; they have their own perspectives and actively influence the people around them with regards to their diet.

Anti-cariogenic. Something that protects against dental caries (tooth decay).

Atopic. An individual is said to be 'atopic' if they have inherited a tendency to develop allergies.

Attention deficit hyperactivity disorder (ADHD). This is a condition in which children (and some adults) find difficulties in concentrating (are inattentive) are physically overactive and impulsive, compared with other children at the same stage of development.

Ayurvedic. Relating to the Ayurveda; ancient Hindu teachings about medicine and health.

Body mass index (BMI). A formula to calculate the proportion of body fat in an individual. The BMI is calculated as weight in kilograms divided by the square of the height in metres (kg/m^2).

Cardiovascular disease. Disease of the heart or blood vessels.

Cross-cutting review. A review of policies that cuts across a number of different government departments.

Dental caries. The formation of cavities in the teeth by the action of bacteria.

Diabetes. Diabetes is a condition where the blood sugar level is higher than normal, which can cause long-term ill health.

Dietary reference values. Dietary reference values (DRVs) are estimates of the amount of energy and nutrients needed by different population groups in the UK.

Dyads. Two individuals regarded as a pair.

Empirical. Knowledge based on observation and experiment.

EpiPen. One of a variety of products available on prescription, which delivers an anti allergic drug through the skin in emergency situations.

Food group. A group of foods, such as butter, margarine and sunflower oil, that contain the same type of nutrients (fats and oils).

Food poverty. 'The inability to obtain healthy, affordable food' (Sustain, 2007).

Foucaultian. In the style of Michel Foucault, a post-structuralist writer.

Globalization. The term 'globalization' describes the increased mobility of goods, services, labour, technology and capital throughout the world. Although globalization is not a new development, its pace has increased with the advent of new technologies, especially in the area of telecommunications (Government of Canada, 2007).

Gross domestic product. A way of measuring a country's economy and a measure of all the goods and services produced by a country in a year.

Homeostasis. The mechanism by which our bodies try to keep internal processes in balance.

Hypothalamus. A part of the brain that is involved in the regulation of certain bodily processes including temperature regulation, water balance, blood sugar and fat metabolism.

Indices of poverty and disadvantage. These are descriptions used to indicate if an individual or family is at social disadvantage. For instance, one sign of poverty may be the receipt of benefits or eligibility for free school meals. Low social class or lack of education are other signs of disadvantage.

Individuation. The process of becoming aware that one is an individual and distinct/separate from others.

Lymph. A clear, almost colourless fluid that contains white blood cells. Lymph travels around the body in a similar way to blood and has its own separate system of lymphatic vessels. It is part of the body's defences against infection.

Macronutrients. Substances such as protein or carbohydrate needed in relatively large amounts to keep us healthy.

Majority world. A term used to describe the two thirds of the world that are less developed than Western countries (the minority world). See Dahlberg et al. (1999) for further discussion.

Malnutrition. A state of poor nutrition resulting from the insufficient or excessive intake of nutrients. Malnutrition can also be caused by an inability to absorb nutrients.

Micronutrients. Substances such as vitamins or minerals that are needed in minute amounts in our diet to keep us healthy.

Morbidity. Illness or disease.

Mortality. Death.

Mortality rate. The numbers of individuals dying from an illness/condition; for example, infant mortality rate.

Neural tube. A tube running along the back of an embryo that will later form the spinal cord and brain.

Nutrient. In the science of nutrition a nutrient is a chemical compound found in food that is used by the body to promote growth and development.

Nutrition transition. The change in diet, resulting from globalization, where the consumption of foods high in fats and sugars is increasing, the consumption of cereals is declining and the intake of fruit and vegetables is inadequate.

Obesity. Being well above the weight expected for one's height. In adults obesity is defined as having a body mass index of over 30 (about 30 lb overweight) but different definitions apply for children.

Obesogenic. A description of anything likely to increase the risk of obesity, for example, an obesogenic diet is one that is energy dense, rich in fat and sugar. An obesogenic lifestyle is one that combines a diet likely to cause obesity with a lack of exercise.

Obsession. An abnormal preoccupation.

Perinatal mortality. The number of stillbirths and deaths of infants around the time of birth per 1,000 births.

Physiological drive. A strong need or desire, such as hunger or desire for sleep, that is the result of internal bodily processes.

Post-structuralist. A point of view that was derived as a reaction against structuralism (see below). In direct contrast to structuralism's claims of culturally independent meaning, post-structuralists typically view culture as inseparable from meaning. In addition, power and discourse are of key importance to post-structuralists such as Foucault (for a fuller discussion, look at Dahlberg et al., 1999).

Pre-eclampsia. A condition in pregnancy that can lead to high blood pressure with a risk of the mother fitting. If untreated the condition can be fatal to both mother and baby.

Public service agreements. Public service agreements (PSAs) set out the key improvements that the public can expect from government expenditure. They are negotiated between each of the main Departments and Her Majesty's Treasury during the spending review process. Each PSA sets out a Department's high-level aim, priority objectives and key outcome-based performance targets (HM Treasury 2007).

Reinforcer. Something that reinforces a behaviour (increases the likelyhood that a behaviour will be repeated). This can be something pleasant such as a reward, or the removal of something that is unpleasant, such as hunger.

Relative poverty. A family can be considered to live in relative poverty if they have sufficient income to meet their *basic* needs but, compared with others around them, have insufficient money to supply other goods and services that are considered 'normal' for the community in which they live. For instance in the UK it is considered normal to have a television and telephone, wear up-to-date clothes and to go away on holiday (Townsend, 1979).

Social anthropology. A branch of anthropology (the scientific study of the origin and behaviour of humans) that deals with human culture and society.

Structuralist. This relates to structuralism, the school of thought that stresses that human actions are guided by concepts and beliefs, and that underlying these are structures of thought which are culturally independent.

References

Acheson, D. (1998) *Independent Inquiry into Inequalities in Health Report*. London: The Stationery Office.

Ainsworth, M., Salter, T. and Russell, L. (1972) *Infant Feeding and Attachment* (ERIC) ED089847.

Albon, D. (2003) 'Treats, transgressions and transformations: the role(s) of sweet eating in six families', unpublished MA, University of Surrey, Roehampton.

Albon, D. (2005) 'Approaches to the study of children, food and sweet-eating: a review of the literature', *Early Child Development and Care*, 175(5): 407–17.

Albon, D. (2006) 'Sweet memories: an examination of six families' narratives around sweet-eating', *Early Childhood Practice*, 8(1): 12–20.

Albon, D. (2007) 'Food for thought: the Importance of food and eating in early childhood practice', in J. Moyles (ed.), *Early Years Foundations: Meeting the Challenge*. Maidenhead: Open University Press.

Alderton, T. and Campbell-Barr, V. (2005) 'Quality early education – quality food and nutrition practices? Some initial results from a pilot research project into food and nutrition practices in early years' settings in Kent, UK', *International Journal of Early Years Education*, 13(3): 197–213.

Altfas, J. (2002) 'Prevalence of attention deficit/hyperactivity disorder among adults in obesity treatment', *BMC Psychiatry*, 2(9). www.biomedcentral.com/1471-244X/2/9 (accessed 30 July 2007).

American Society for Reproductive Medicine (2001) *Patients' Fact Sheet: Weight and Fertility*. Birmingham: AL: ASRM.

Anning, A., Cottrell, D. Frost, N., Green, J. and Robinson, M. (2006) *Developing Multi-professional Teamwork for Integrated Children's Services*. Maidenhead: Open University Press.

Atkinson, R., Atkinson, R., Smith, E., Bem, D. and Nolen-Hoeksema, S. (1996) *Hilgard's Introduction to Psychology*. Orland, FL: Harcourt Brace.

Atree, P. (2006) 'A critical analysis of UK public health policies in relation to diet and nutrition in low income families', *Maternal and Child Nutrition*, 2: 67–78.

Barthes, R. (1975) 'Towards a psychosociology of contemporary food consumption', in E. Forster and R. Forster (eds), *European Diet from Pre-Industrial to Modern Times*. New York: Harper Row.

Bartley, M. (2004) 'Using international comparisons to understand health inequality', paper presented at the Centre for Census and Survey Research; Research Methods Festival, July.

BBC (2003) 'Baby death nursery fined', *BBC News*, http://news.bbc.co.uk/2/hi/uk_news/england/ds/bucks/herts/3226675.stm (accessed 25 July 2007).

BBC, www.bbc.co.uk/health/healthy_living/nutrition/ (accessed 25 July 2007).

Beattie, A. (2001) 'Health promoting schools as learning organisations', in A. Scriven and J. Orme (eds), *Health Promotion: Professional Perspectives*, 2nd edn. Houndmills: Palgrave.

Ben-Ari, E. (1997) *Body Projects in Japanese Childcare: Culture, Organisation and Emotions in a Preschool*. Richmond: Curzon Press.

Black, D., Morris, J., Smith, C. and Townsend, P. (1980) *Inequalities in Health: Report of a research Working Group*. London: Department of Health and Social Security, www.sochealth.co.uk/history/black.htm (accessed 28 July 2007).

Block, R., Krebs, N. and the Committee on Child Abuse and Neglect and the Committee on Nutrition (2005) 'Failure to thrive as a manifestation of child neglect', *Pediatrics*, 116(5): 1234–7.

Bourdieu, P. (1986) *Distinction: A Social Critique of Judgement and Taste*. London: Routledge and Kegan Paul.

Bowlby, J. (1969) *Attachment and Loss: Attachment*, vol. 1. Harmondsworth: Penguin.

Bradby, H. (1997) 'Glaswegian Punjabi women's thinking about food', in P. Caplan (ed.), *Food, Health and Identity*. London: Routledge.

Braun, D. (1992) 'Working with parents', in G. Pugh (ed.), *Contemporary Issues in the Early Years*. London: Paul Chapman Publishing.

Bretherton, I. (1992) 'The origins of attachment theory: John Bowlby and Mary Ainsworth', *Developmental Psychology*, 28: 759–75.

British Medical Association (BMA) (1999) *Growing up in Britain: Ensuring a Healthy Future for our Children*. London: BMA Publications.

British Medical Association (BMA) Board of Science (2005) *Preventing Childhood Obesity*. London: BMA Publications.

British Nursing News On Line (2006) www.bnn-online.co.uk/news_datesearch.asp? SearchDate=26/Sep/2003&Year=2003 (accessed 25 July 2007).

British Nutrition Foundation (BNF) (2004) *Nutrition Basics*. London: British Nutrition Foundation, www.nutrition.org.uk/ (accessed 25 July 2007).

British Nutrition Foundation (BNF) (2007) *Nutrient Requirements and Recommendations*, www.nutrition.org.uk/home.asp?siteId=43&sectionId=414&parentSection=320& which=1 (accessed 25 July 2007).

Britton, J., Britton, H. and Gronwaldt, V. (2006) 'Breastfeeding, sensitivity, and attachment', *Pediatrics*, 118(5): 1436–43.

Brooks, S., Mitchell, A. and Steffenson, N. (2000) 'Mothers, infants, and DHA: implications for nursing practice', *American Journal of Maternal Child Nursing*, 25(2): 71–5.

Bryant-Waugh, R. and Lask, B. (1995) 'Eating disorders in children', *Journal of Child Psychology and Psychiatry and Allied Disciplines*, 36(3): 191–202.

Burke, L. (2002) 'Healthy eating in the school environment – a holistic approach', *International Journal of Consumer Studies*, 26(2): 159–63.

Buttriss, J. (2003) 'Healthy start: proposals on reform to the welfare food scheme', *Nutrition Bulletin*, 28(1): 35–6.

Buttriss, J. (2005) 'Government promises school meals will be transformed', *Nutrition Bulletin*, 30(3): 211–14.

Buttriss, J. and Stanner, S. (2005) 'Revitalising school food and other topical issues', *Nutrition Bulletin*, 30(4): 305–6.

Caplan, P. (1994) Feasts, fasts, famine: food for thought, *Berg Occasional Papers in Anthropology*, no. 2, Oxford: Berg.

Caplan, P. (1997) 'Approaches to food, health and identity' in P. Caplan (ed.), *Food, Health and Identity*. London: Routledge.

Cardwell, M., Clark, L. and Meldrum, C. (1998) *Psychology for A level*. London: Collins Educational.

Caroline Walker Trust (Expert Working Group) (2006) *Eating Well for Under Fives in Child Care: Practical and Nutritional Guidelines*, (2nd ed), St Austell: Caroline Walker Trust.

Cashdan, E. (1998) 'Adaptiveness of food and learning and food aversions in children', *Social Science Information*, 37: 613–32.

Chamberlain, K. (2004) 'Food and health: expanding the agenda for health psychology', *Journal of Health Psychology*, 9(4): 467–82.

Charles, N. and Kerr, M. (1986) 'Eating properly, the family and state benefit', *Sociology*, 20(3): 412–29.

Central Intelligence Agency (CIA) (2007) *The World Fact Book Rank Order GDP per capita*, www.cia.gov/cia/publications/factbook/rankorder/2004rank.html (accessed 28 July 2007).

Centres for Disease Control and Prevention (2005) *WHO: Which Mothers Are Most Likely to Deliver Infants of Low Birth Weight?* www.cdc.gov/pednss/how_to/interpret_data/case_studies/low_birthweight/who.htm (accessed 30 July 2007).

Cheater, S. (2001) 'Pupil snacks: the extent to which food and drink policies in Wirral schools promote health', *Health Education Journal*, 60(4): 303–12.

Chief Medical Officer of Health (CMO) (2005) *Meeting the Need for Vitamin D. CMO Update. Summer 2005*. London: Department of Health.

Children Act 2004, London: HMSO.

Clark, A., Kjorholt, A.T. and Moss, P. (eds) (2005) *Beyond Listening: Children's Perspectives on Early Childhood Services*. Bristol: Policy Press.

Cohen, E. (2007) *ADHD Drug Use for Youth Obesity Raises Ethical Questions*. CNN.Com, www.cnn.com/2007/HEALTH/03/21/vs.adderall/ (accessed 28 July 2007).

Consultative Group on Early Childcare and Development (CGECD) (1989) *A Developmental Classification of Feeding Disorders in the First Six Months of Life*. Washington: CGECD.

Council for Disabled Children (2004) *The Dignity of Risk*. London: NCB.

Counihan, C. and Van-Esterik, P. (1997) 'Introduction', in C. Counihan, P. Van-Esterik (eds), *Food and Culture: A Reader*. London: Routledge.

Dahlberg, G. and Moss, P. (2005) *Ethics and Politics in Early Childhood Education*. Abingdon: Routledge/Falmer.

Dahlberg, G., Moss, P. and Pence, A. (1999) *Beyond Quality in Early Childhood Education and Care: Postmodern Perspectives*. London: Falmer Press.

Dani, J., Burrill, C. and Demming-Adams, B. (2005) 'The remarkable role of nutrition in learning and behaviour', *Nutrition and Food Science*, 35(4): 258–63.

Deckelbaum, R. (2002) *Nutrition Today Matters Tomorrow: A Report from the March of Dimes Task Force on Optimal Human Development*. March of Dimes. www.marchofdimes.com/aboutus/791_1622.asp (accessed 14 October 2007).

Dehgan, M., Akhtar-Danesh, N. and Merchant, A. (2005) 'Childhood obesity, prevalence and prevention', *Nutrition Journal*, 4(24): 1–8.

Delamont, S. (1995) *Appetites and Identities*. London: Routledge.

Department for Education and Employment (DfEE) (1998) *Excellence in Schools*. London: DfEE.

Department for Education and Skills (DfES) (2003) *Every Child Matters*, CM 5860. Norwich: HMSO.

Department for Education and Skills (DfES) (2008) *The Early Years Foundation Stage: Setting the Standards for Learning, Development and Care for Children from Birth to Five*. Nottingham: DfES Publications.

Department of Health (DoH) (1999) *Saving Lives: Our Healthier Nation*. London: Stationery Office.

Department of Health (DoH) (2004a) *HIV and Infant Feeding*. London: DoH Publications.

Department of Health (DoH) (2004b) *Spending Review Public Service Agreements*. London: HM Treasury.

Department of Health (DoH) (2004c) *Choosing Health, Making Healthier Choices Easier, White Paper*. London: The Stationery office.

Department of Health (DoH) (2005) *The Health Survey of England 2004: Updating of Trend Tables to include 2004 Data*. London: The Stationery Office.

Department of Health (DoH) (2006a) *Measuring Childhood Obesity: Guidance for Primary Care Trusts*. London: DoH.

Department of Health (DoH) (2006b) *Health Profile of England*. London: DoH.

Department of Health (DoH) (2007a) *Advice on Infant Milks Based on Goats Milk*. London: DoH.

Department of Health (DoH) (2007b) *Alcohol and Pregnancy,* www.dh.gov.uk/en/News/DH_074968 (accessed 25 July 2007).

Department of Health (DoH) (2007c) *The Pregnancy Book*. London: DoH.

Department of Work and Pensions (DWP) (2006) *Making a Difference: Tackling Poverty a Progress Report*, London: DWP. www.dwp.gov.uk/publications/dwp/2006/poverty/tackling-poverty.pdf (accessed 16 October 2007).

Department of Work and Pensions (DWP) (2007) *Working for Children*. London: The Stationery Office. www.dwp.gov.uk/publications/dwp/2007/childpoverty/childpoverty.pdf (accessed 28 July 2007).

DeVault, M. (1997) 'Conflict and deference', in C. Counihan and P. Van-Esterik (eds), *Food and Culture: A Reader*. London: Routledge.

Dixon, J. and Banwell, C. (2004) 'Heading the table: parenting and the junior consumer', *British Food Journal*, 106(3): 181–93.

Douglas, M. (1997) 'Deciphering a meal', in C. Counihan and P. Van-Esterik (eds), *Food and Culture: A Reader*. London: Routledge.

Economic and Social Research Council (ESRC) (2006) *International Fact Sheet: Global poverty*, www.esrc.ac.uk/ESRCInfoCentre/index.aspx (accessed 28 July 2007).

Ekstrom, M. (1991) 'Class and gender in the kitchen' in E.L Furst, R. Prattala, M. Ekstrom, L. Holm and U. Kjaernes (eds), *Palatable Worlds*. Oslo: Solum Forlag.

Elfer, P., Goldschmeid, E. and Selleck, D. (2003) *Key Person Relationships in Nursery*. London: Sage.

Eliot, E. (2007) *We're Not Robots: The Voices of Daycare Providers*. Albany, NY: State University of New York Press.

Elliott, J. (2007) 'The big millennium babies: quarter are overweight', *Times on line*, 10 June.

Ellis, L., Hillier, F. and Summerbell, C. (2006) *A Systematic Review of the Effect of Nutrition, Diet and Dietary Change on Learning, Education and Performance of Children of Relevance to UK Schools*. Middlesbrough: University of Teesside School of Health and Social Care.

Ellis, R. (1983) 'The way to a man's heart: food in the violent home', in A. Murcott (ed.), *The Sociology of Food and Eating*. Aldershot: Gower.

Eysenck, M. (2004) *Psychology: An International Perspective*. London: Psychology Press.

Falk, P. (1991) 'The sweetness of forbidden fruit: towards an anthropology of taste', in E.L Furst, R. Prattala, M. Ekstrom, L. Holm and U. Kjaernes (eds), *Palatable Worlds*. Oslo: Solum Forlag.

Fiddes, N. (1997) 'Declining meat: past, present … and future imperfect?' in P. Caplan (ed.), *Food, Health and Identity*. London: Routledge.

Fischler, C. (1988) 'Food, self and identity', *Social Science Information*, 27(2): 275–92.

Fitchen, J. (1997) 'Hunger, malnutrition, and poverty in the contemporary United States', in C. Counihan and P. Van-Esterik (eds), *Food and Culture: A Reader*. London: Routledge.

Food Standards Agency (FSA) (2001) 'Members of new Scientific Advisory Committee on Nutrition approve', press release 22 February.

Food Standards Agency (FSA) (2006a) *Food Allergy: How to Avoid Certain Foods*. London: Food Standards Agency.

Food Standards Agency (FSA) (2006b) *Food Intolerance and Coeliac Disease*. London: Food Standards Agency.

Food Standards Agency (FSA) (2007a) 'Agency revises advice on certain artificial food colours', www.food.gov.uk/news/newsarchive/2007/sep/foodcolours (accessed 06 September 2007).

Food Standards Agency (FSA) (2007b) Eatwell web site, www.eatwell.gov.uk (accessed 4 October 2007).

Foucault, M. (1977) *Discipline and Punishment*. London: Allen Lane.

Giddens, A. (1991) *Modernity and Self Identity: Self and Society in the Late Modern Age*. Cambridge: Polity Press.

Giovanni, D. (2006) 'The pleasure of eating', *Children in Europe* (10): 10–11.

Glewwe, P., Jacoby, H. and King, E. (2001) 'Early childhood nutrition and academic achievement: a longitudinal analysis', *Journal of Public Economics*, 81: 345–68.

Golden, D. (2005) 'Nourishing the nation: the uses of food in an Israeli kindergarten', *Food and Foodways*, 13: 181–99.

Goldin, J. (2007) Statement to the press, 17 July.

Goldschmeid, E. and Jackson, S. (2002) *People Under Three, Young Children in Daycare*. London: Routledge.

Government of Canada (2007) *Economic Concepts Globalization*, www.canadianeconomy.gc.ca/english/economy/globalization.html (accessed 28 July 2007).

Great Ormond Street Hospital Trust (GOSHT) (2007) *Clinical Guidance Procedure; Infant Formula*. London: GOSHT. website: www.ich.ucl.ac.uk/(accessed 14 October 2007)

Greenman, J. and Stonehouse, A. (1997) *Prime Times: A Handbook for Excellence in Infant and Teacher Programs*. Melbourne: Longman.

Grieshaber, S. (1997) 'Mealtime rules: power and resistance in the construction of meal-time rules', *British Journal of Sociology*, 48(4): 649–66.

Graham, H. and Power, C. (2004) *Childhood Disadvantage and Adult Health: a Lifecourse Framework*. London: Health Development Agency.

Gustafsson, U. (2003) 'School meals policy: the problem with governing children', in E. Dowler and C. Jones-Finer (eds), *The Welfare of Food: Rights and Responsibilities in a Changing World*. Oxford: Blackwell.

Hackett, A. (2006) *A Short History of Nutrition*. Liverpool: Consumer Studies Department at Liverpool John Moores University.

Haines, L., Rogers, J. and Dobson, P. (2000) 'A study of drinking facilities in schools', *Nursing Times*, 96(40): 2–4.

Harvard School of Public Health (2006) *Food Pyramids, What You Should Really Eat*; www.hsph.harvard.edu/nutritionsource/pyramids.html (accessed 25 July 2007).

Hawks, C. (2006) 'Uneven dietary development: linking the policies and processes of globalization with the nutrition transistion, obesity and diet-related chronic diseases' in *Globalization and Health*. www.globalization and health.com/content/2/1/4 (accessed 12 October 2007).

HM Treasury (2007) *Acronym Buster: What are PSAs?* www.hm-treasury.gov.uk/documents/public_spending_reporting/public_service_performance/psr_performance_efficiency_acronym_buster.cfm (accessed 28 July 2007).

Horowitz, M., Feinle-Bisset, C. and Little, T.J. (2005) 'Role of Cholecystokinin in appetite control and body weight regulation', *Obesity Reviews*, 6(4): 297–306.

House of Commons Public Accounts Committee (HCPAC) (2007) *Tackling Child Obesity, First Steps*. London: The Stationery Office.

Hughes, M.H. (1997) 'Soul, black women, and food', in C. Counihan and P. Van-Esterik (eds), *Food and Culture: A Reader*. London: Routledge.

Humphreys, C. (2001) 'The impact of domestic violence on children', in P. Foley, J. Roche and S. Tucker (eds), *Children in Society: Contemporary Theory, Policy and Practice*. Houndmills: Palgrave.

Hyder, T. and Mukherji, P. (2004) *Aspects of Health Promotion: Distance Learning Handbook.* London: London Metropolitan University.

Information Centre for Health and Social Care (2007) *Infant Feeding Survey 2005: Summary.* London: The Information Centre.

Jackson, A. and Robinson, S. (2001) 'Dietary guidelines for pregnancy: a review of current evidence', *Public Health and Nutrition,* 4(2): 625–30.

Jagger, E. (2000) 'Consumer bodies', in P. Hancock, B. Hughes, E. Jagger, K. Paterson, R. Russell, E. Tulle-Winton and M. Tyler (eds), *The Body, Culture and Society: An Introduction.* Buckingham: Open University Press.

James, A. (1990) 'The good, the bad and the delicious: the role of confectionery in British society', *The Sociological Review,* 38(4): 666–88.

James, A. (1997) 'How British is British food?', in P. Caplan (ed.), *Food, Health and Identity.* London: Routledge.

James, A. (1998) 'Confections, concoctions and conceptions', in H. Jenkins (ed.), *The Children's Culture Reader.* New York: New York University Press.

Jonsson, I.M., Hallberg, L.R.-M. and Gustafsson, I.-B. (2002) 'Cultural foodways in Sweden: repeated focus group interviews with Somalian women', *International Journal of Consumer Studies,* 26(4): 328–39.

Jotangia, D., Moody, A., Stamatakis, E. and Wardle, H. (2006) *Obesity Among Children Under 11.* London: National Statistics.

Judd, K., Platt, S., Costongs, C. and Jurczak, K. (2006) *Health Inequalities: A Challenge for Europe.* London: Department of Health.

Kelly, Y., Watt, R. and Nazroo, J. (2006) 'Racial/ethnic differences in breastfeeding initiation and continuation in the United Kingdom and comparison with findings in the United States', *Pediatrics,* 118(5): 1428–35.

King, J. (2006) 'Maternal obesity, metabolism and pregnancy outcomes', *Annual Review of Nutrition,* 26: 271–91.

Kjorholt, A.T. (2005) 'The competent child and the 'right to be oneself': reflections on children as fellow citizens in an early childhood centre', in A. Clark, A.T. Kjorholt and P. Moss (eds), *Beyond Listening: Children's Perspectives on Early Childhood Services.* Bristol: Policy Press.

Kuo, L., Kitlinska, J., Tilan, J., Li, L., Baker, S., Johnson, M., Lee, E., Burnett, M., Fricke, S., Kvetnansky, R., Herzog, H. and Zukowska, Z. (2007) 'Neuropeptide Y acts directly in the periphery on fat tissue and mediates stress-induced obesity and metabolic syndrome', *Nature Medicine,* published online: 1 July 2007, doi> 10.1038/nm1611.

Laitinen, J., Ek, E. and Sovio, U. (2002) 'Stress related eating and drinking behaviour and body mass index and predictors of this behaviour', *Preventive Medicine,* 34: 29–39.

Levi-Strauss, C. (1966) 'The culinary triangle', *New Society,* December: 937–40.

Lindata (2006) *Growth Monitoring Data for Nurses, Midwives, Health Visitors and Practice Teachers,* www.lindata.info/index.html (accessed 25 July 2007).

Lindberg, L., Bohlin, G., Hagekull, B. and Palmerus, K. (1998) 'Interactions between mothers and infants showing food refusal', *Infant Mental Health Journal,* 17(4): 334–47.

Lindon, J. (2006) *Equality in Early Childhood: Linking Theory and Practice.* Abingdon: Hodder Arnold.

Ludvigsen, A. and Sharma, N. (2004) *Burger Boy and Sporty Girl: Children and Young People's Attitudes Towards Food in School.* Ilford: Barnardos.

Lumeng, J. (2005) 'What can we do to prevent childhood obesity?', *Zero to Three,* 25(3b): 13–19.

Lupton, D. (1994) 'Food memory and meaning: the symbolic and social nature of food events', *The Sociological Review,* 42(4): 664–85.

Lupton, D. (1996) *Food, the Body and the Self.* London: Sage.

Mackenback, J. (2006) *Health Inequalities, Europe in Profile*. London: Department of Health.

Majumdar, B. (2005) 'Junk food, no play makes city kids fat', *The Telegraph Calcutta*, 7 May www.telegraphindia.com/1050527/asp/calcutta/story_4790049.asp (accessed 30 July 2007).

Manning-Morton, J. (2006) 'The personal is professional: professionalism and the birth to threes practitioner', *Contemporary Issues in Early Childhood*, 7(1): 42–52.

Manning-Morton, J. and Thorp, M. (2003) *Key Times for Play: The First Three Years*. Maidenhead: Open University Press.

Marano, H. (2006) 'Stress and eating', *Psychology Today*, www.psychologytoday.com/ (accessed 28 July 2007).

Marchi, M. and Cohen, P. (1990) 'Early childhood eating behaviors and adolescent eating disorders', *Journal of the American Academy of Child and Adolescent Psychiatry*, 29(1): 112–17.

Markku, S., Sandler, D.P., Hoppin, J., Blair, A. and Baird, D.D. (2006) 'Reduced fertility among overweight and obese men', *Epidemiology*, 17(5): 520–3.

Marks, D., Murray, M., Evans, B., Willig, C., Woodall, C. and Sykes, C. (2005) *Health Psychology: Theory, Research and Practice*. London: Sage.

Markwell, S. and Speller, V. (2001) 'Partnership working and interprofessional collaboration: policy and practice', in A. Scriven and J. Orme (eds), *Health Promotion: Professional Perspectives*, 2nd edn. Houndmills: Palgrave.

Martens, L. and Warde, A. (1997) 'Urban pleasure? On the meaning of eating out in a northern city, in A. Murcott (ed.), *Food, Health and Identity*. London: Routledge.

Martin, R., Ben-Shlomo, Y., Gunnell, D., Elwood, P., Yarnell, J. and Davey Smith, G. (2005) 'Breast feeding and cardiovascular disease risk factors, incidence and mortality: the Caerphilly study', *Journal of Epidemiology and Community Health*, 59: 121–9.

Martins, Y. (2006) 'Dietary experiences and food acceptance patterns from infancy through early childhood', *Food, Culture and Society*, 9(3): 287–98.

McAuliffe, A.M. and Lane, J. (2005) *Listening and Responding to Young Children's Views on Food*. London: National Children's Bureau.

McIntosh, W.A. and Zey, M. (1989) 'Women as gatekeepers of food consumption: a sociological critique', *Food and Foodways*, 3(4): 317–32.

Meigs, A. (1997) 'Food as a cultural construction', in C. Counihan and P. Van-Esterik (eds), *Food and Culture: A Reader*. London: Routledge.

Mennell, S., Murcott, A. and Van-Otterloo, A.H. (1992) *The Sociology of Eating, Diet and Culture*. London: Sage.

Mental Health Foundation (2007) *Child Eating Disorder Treatments Rise by a Third*, www.mentalhealth.org.uk/information/news/ (accessed 28 July 2007).

Mitchell, W. and Green, E. (2002) 'I don't know what I'd do without my mam': motherhood, identity and support networks', *The Sociological Review*, 50(1): 1–22.

Molyneux, J. (2001) 'Interprofessional teamworking: what makes teams work well?' *Journal of Interprofessional Care*, 15(1): 29–35.

Moore, H., Nelson, P., Marshall, J., Cooper, M., Zambas, H., Brewster, K. and Atkin, K. (2005) 'Laying the foundations for health: food provision for under-fives day care', *Appetite*, 44: 107–213.

Moran, V. (2007) 'A systematic review of dietary assessments of pregnant adolescents in industrialized countries', *British Journal of Nutrition*, 97: 411–25.

Morgan, K. (2007) *School Food and the Public Domain: The Politics of the Public Plate*, www.cf.ac.uk/cplan/ri/publications/publicplate.pdf (accessed 10 April 2007).

Moynihan, P. (2000) 'Foods and factors that protect against dental caries', *Nutrition Bulletin*, 25(4): 281–6.

Moynihan, P. (2005) 'The role of diet and nutrition in the etiology and prevention of oral diseases', *Bulletin of the World Health Organization*, 83(9): 694–9.

Mukherji, P. (2001) *Understanding Children's Challenging Behaviour*. Cheltenham: Nelson Thornes.

Mukherji, P. (2005) 'The importance of health', in L. Dryden, R. Forbes, P. Mukherji and L. Pound (eds), *Essential Early Years*. London: Hodder Arnold.

Muñoz, K. and Jeris, L. (2005) 'Learning to be interdisciplinary: an action research approach to boundary spanning', *Health Education Journal*, 64(1): 5–12.

Murcott, A. (1988) 'Sociological and social anthropological approaches to food and eating', *World Review of Nutrition and Diet*, 55: 1–40.

Murphy, E., Parker, S. and Phipps, C. (1998) 'Competing agendas in infant feeding', *British Food Journal*, 100(3): 128–32.

Mustillo, S., Worthman, C., Erkanli, A., Keeler, M., Angol, A. and Costello, J. (2003) 'Obesity and psychiatric disorder: developmental trajectories', *Pediatrics*, 112(4): 851–9.

Naidoo, J. and Wills, J. (2000) *Health Promotion: Foundations for Practice*, 2nd edn. Edinburgh: Bailliere Tindall.

National Alliance for Equity in Dental Health (NAEDH) (2000) *Inequalities in Dental Health; A briefing Paper*. Manchester: British Fluoridation Society.

NCH (2004) *Going hungry, the struggle to eat healthily on a low income.* www.nch.org.uk/uploads/documents/going_hungrymainreport2.pdf (accessed 14 October 2007).

Nederkoorn, C., Braet, C., Van Eijs, Y., Tanghe, A. and Jansen, A. (2006) 'Why obese children cannot resist food: the role of impulsivity', *Eating Behaviours*, 7: 315–22.

Nelson, M. (2000) 'Childhood nutrition and poverty', *Proceedings of the Nutrition Society*, 59: 307–15.

Newton, G. (2006) *The Aging Population*, Welcome Trust, www.wellcome.ac.uk/doc_WTX033811.html (accessed 28 July 2007).

NHS Health Scotland (2004) *Adventures in Foodland: Ideas for Making Food Fun from an Early Age*. Edinburgh: Health Scotland.

Noorani, S. (2005) 'Food in schools: update', *Nutrition Bulletin*, 30(3): 278–81.

O'Brien, K., Donangelo, C., Vargas Zapata, C., Abrams, K., Martin Spencer, F. and King, J. (2006) 'Bone calcium turnover during pregnancy and lactation in women with low calcium diets is associated with calcium intake and circulating insulin-like growth factor 1 concentrations', *American Journal of Clinical Nutrition*, 83(2): 317–23.

Oates, R. (1984) 'Non organic failure to thrive', *Australian Paediatric Journal*, 20(2): 95–100.

Oxfam (2002) 'Aids and hunger, South Africa's twin killers', press release 28 November.

Papamandjaris, A. (2000) *Breakfast and Learning in Children: A Review of the Effects of Breakfast on Scholastic Performance*, report prepared for Breakfast for Learning, Canadian Living Foundation.

Passmore, S. and Harris, G. (2004) 'Education, health and school meals: a review of policy changes in England and Wales over the last century', *Nutrition Bulletin*, 29(3): 221–7.

Petrie, S. and Owen, S. (2005) *Authentic Relationships in Group Care for Infants and Toddlers – Resources for Infant Educarers (RIE): Principles into Practice*. London: Jessica Kingsley.

Pine, K. (2001) 'Children's perceptions of body shape: a thinness bias in pre-adolescent girls and associations with femininity', *Clinical Child Psychology and Psychiatry*, 6(4): 519–36.

Pinkerton, J. (2001) 'Developing partnership practice', in P. Foley, J. Roche and S. Tucker (eds), *Children in Society: Contemporary Theory, Policy and Practice*. Houndmills: Palgrave.

Piperakis, S.M., Sotitiou, A., Georgiou, E., Thanou, A. and Zafiropoulou, M. (2004) 'Understanding nutrition: a study of Greek primary school children's dietary habits, before and after nutritional intervention', *Journal of Science Education and Technology*, 13(1): 129–36.

Ramachandran, P. (2004) 'Breast feeding practices in South Asia', *Indian Journal of Medical Research*, 119(6): 13–15.

Ray, S., Mishra, M., Biswas, R., Kumar, S., Halder, A. and Chatterjee, T. (1999) 'Nutritional status of pavement dweller children of Calcutta City', *Indian Journal of Public Health*, 43(1): 49–54.

Rayner, M. and Scarborough, P. (2005) 'The burden of food related ill health in the UK', *Journal of Epidemiology and Community Health*, 59: 1054–7.

Richardson, L. (2000) 'Writing: a method of inquiry', in N.K. Denzin and Y.S. Lincoln (eds), *Handbook of Qualitative Research*, 2nd edn. London: Sage.

Rivkin, M.S. (2007) 'Keeping fit in body and mind', *Early Childhood Today*, 21(5): 28–36.

Robinson, P. (2000) 'Eating disorders: essential information', *Student British Medical Journal*, 8: 175–216.

Robinson, S. (2000) 'Children's perceptions of who controls their food', *Human Nutrition and Dietetics*, 13: 163–71.

Robinson, S. (2006) *Healthy Eating in Primary Schools*. London: Paul Chapman Publishing.

Roos, G. (2002) 'Our bodies are made of pizza – food and embodiment among children in Kentucky', *Ecology of Food and Nutrition*, 41: 1–19.

Rose, R. and Falconer, P. (1992) 'Individual taste or collective decision? Public policy on school meals', *Journal of Social Policy*, 21(3): 349–73.

Royal College of Psychiatrists (RCOP) (2004) *Eating Disorders in Young People. Fact sheet for Parents and Teachers*. London: RCOP.

Ruston, D., Hoare, J., Henderson, L., Gregory, J., Bates, C.J., Prentice, A., Birch, M., Swan, G. and Farron, M. (2004) *The National Diet and Nutrition Survey: Adults Aged 19–64 Years. Volume 4: Nutritional Status (Anthropometry and Blood Analyses), Blood Pressure and Physical Activity*. London: The Stationery Office.

Satter, E. (1992) 'The feeding relationship', *Zero to Three*, www.zerotothree.org/site/Page Server?pagename=ter_key_health_satter&AddInterest=1147 (accessed 28 July 2007).

School Meals Review Panel (2005) *Turning the Tables: Transforming School Food*. London: School Meals Review Panel.

School Food Trust (2007) *A Guide to the Government's New Food Based Standards for School Lunches*. Sheffield: School Food Trust.

Scottish Executive (2002) *Hungry for Success: A Whole School Approach to School Meals in Scotland*. Edinburgh: Scottish Executive.

Scriven, A. and Stiddard, L. (2003) 'Empowering schools: translating health promotion principles into practice', *Health Education*, 103(2): 110–18.

Sebire, N.J., Jolly, M., Harris, J.P., Wadsworth, J., Joffe, M., Bear, R.W., Regan, L. and Robinson, S. (2001) 'Maternal obesity and pregnancy outcome: a study of 287,213 pregnancies in London', *International Journal of Obstetrics and Related Metabolic Disorders*, 25(8): 1175–82.

Seiter, E. (1998) 'Children's desires/mothers' dilemmas: the social context of consumption', in H. Jenkins (ed.), *The Children's Culture Reader*. New York: New York University Press.

Sellers, K., Russo, T.J., Baker, I. and Dennison, B.A. (2005) 'The role of childcare providers in the prevention of childhood overweight', *Journal of Early Childhood Research*, 3(3): 227–42.

Sepp, H., Abrahamsson, L. and Fjellstrom, C. (2006) 'Pre-school staff's attitudes toward foods in relation to the pedagogic meal', *International Journal of Consumer Studies*, 30(2): 224–32.

Sharp, I. (1992) *Nutritional Guidelines for School Meals*. London: Caroline Walker Trust.

Sicherer, S., Munoz-Furlong, A., Murphy, R., Wood, R. and Sampson, H. (2003) 'Symposium: pediatric food allergy', *Pediatrics*, 111(6): 1591–4.

Singer, P. (1975) *Animal Liberation: A New Ethics for the Treatment of Animals*. New York: Avon.

Sjoberg, R., Nilsson, K. and Leppert, J. (2005) 'Obesity, shame, and depression in school aged children: a population based study', *Pediatrics*, 116(3): 389–92.

Sjostrom, L. (2004) 'Lifestyle, diabetes, and cardiovascular risk factors 10 years after bariatric surgery', *New England Journal of Medicine*, 351(26): 2683–93.

Skinner, J., Bounds, W., Carruth, B., Morris, M. and Zeigler, P. (2004) 'Predictors of children's body mass index: a longitudinal study of diet and growth of children aged 2–8y.', *International Journal of Obesity*, 28: 477–86.

Sobo, E.J. (1997) 'The sweetness of fat: health, procreation and sociability in rural Jamaica', in C. Counihan and P. Van-Esterik (eds), *Food and Culture: A Reader*. London: Routledge.

Stanner, S. (2004) 'Improving nursery menus without parent protest', *Nutrition Bulletin*, 29: 6–7.

Steedman, C. (1990) *Childhood, Culture and Class in Britain: Margaret McMillan 1860–1931*. London: Virago.

Stevenson, J. (2006) 'Dietary influences on cognitive development and behaviour in children', *Proceedings of the Nutrition Society*, 65: 361–5.

Strauss, S. (2006) 'Clara M. Davis and the wisdom of letting children choose their own diets', *Canadian Medical Association Journal*, 175(10): 1199–1201.

Stubbs, C. and Lee, A. (2004) 'The obesity epidemic; both energy intake and physical activity contribute', *Medical Journal of Australia*, 181: 489–91.

Sustain (2007) *What is Food Poverty?* www.sustainweb.org/page.php?id=187 (accessed 28 July 2007).

Swinburn, B. and Egger, G. (2002) 'Preventative strategies against weight gain and obesity', *Obesity Reviews*, 3(4): 289–301.

Thurtle, V. (1998) 'Growth and development', in J. Taylor and M. Woods (eds), *Early Childhood Studies an Holistic Approach*. London: Arnold.

Tidy, C. (2007) *Anorexia Nervosa*, UK Patient Plus, www.patient.co.uk/showdoc/40000626/ (accessed 28 July 2007).

Tones, K. (2001) 'Health promotion: the empowerment imperative', in A. Scriven and J. Orme (eds), *Health Promotion: Professional Perspectives*, 2nd edn. Houndmills: Palgrave.

Townsend, P. (1979) *Poverty in the United Kingdom*. Harmondsworth: Penguin.

Townsend, P. and Davidson, N. (1982) *Inequalities in Health*. (Black report). Harmondsworth: Penguin.

The Consultative Group on Early Childcare and Development (1989) *A Developmental Classification of Feeding Disorders in the First Six Months of Life* Washington: CGECD.

Trichopoulou, A. (2005) 'Modified Mediterranean diet and survival: EPIC elderly prospective cohort study', *British Medical Journal*, 330(7498): 991–5.

Underdown, A. (2007) *Young Children's Health and Well-Being*. Maidenhead: Open University Press.

United Nations (UN) (2006) *Human Development Report: Inequality in Income or Expenditure 2006*, Table 15. http://hdr.undp.org/hdr2006/pdfs/report/HDR_2006_Tables.pdf (accessed 28 July 2007).

United Nations Children's Fund (UNICEF) www.unicef.org.uk (accessed 25 July 2007).

United Nations Children's Fund (UNICEF) (2006) *UNICEF Baby Friendly Initiative: Health Benefits of Breastfeeding*. London: UNICEF.

US Department of Agriculture (2007) www.mypyramid.gov/ (accessed 25 July 2007).

Valentine, G. (1999) 'Eating in: home, consumption and identity', *The Sociological Review*, 47(3): 491–524.

Van Bever, H.P., Docx, M. and Stevens, W.J. (1986) 'Food and food additives in severe atopic dermatitis', *Allergy*, 44(8): 588–94.

Viner, R. and Cole, T. (2005) 'Adult socioeconomic, educational, social and psychological outcomes of childhood obesity: a national birth cohort study', *British Medical Journal*, www.bmj.com/cgi/content/abridged/330/7504/1354 (accessed 25 July 2007).

Viruru, R. (2001) *Early Childhood Education: Postcolonial Perspectives from India*. London: Sage.

Wallbank, J.A. (2001) *Challenging Motherhood(s)*. Harlow: Pearson Education.

Ward, A., Ramsey, R., Turnbull, S., Steele, M., Steele, H. and Treasure, A. (2001) 'Attachment in anorexia nervosa: a transgenerational perspective', *British Journal of Medical Psychology*, 74(4): 497–505.

Weaver, M. (2006) 'Parents and head in school dinner talk', *Guardian Unlimited*, 18 September http://education.guardian.co.uk/schoolmeals/story/0,,1875343,00.html (accessed 30 July 2007).

Wessien, A., Sepp, H. and Fjellstrom, C. (2002) 'Swedish preschool children's experience of food', *International Journal of Consumer Studies*, 26(4): 264–71.

Wired for Health (2007) www.wiredforhealth.gov.uk/doc.php?docid=7267 (accessed 25 July 2007).

Wood, R. (2003) 'The natural history of food allergy', *Paediatrics*, 111(6): 1631–7.

World Bank (2001) *World Development Report 2000/2001*. Washington, DC: World Bank.

World Health Organization (WHO) (1986) *Ottawa Charter for Health Promotion*. Geneva: WHO.

World Health Organization (WHO) (2003) *Global Strategy for Infant and Young Child Feeding*. Geneva: WHO.

World Health Organization (WHO) (2005a) *World Health Organization and the Millennium Development Goals*, www.who.int/mediacentre/factsheets/fs290/en/index.html (accessed 28 July 2007).

World Health Organization (WHO) (2005b) *World Health Organization Global report 2005*, http://www.who.int/whr/2005/overview/en/index.html (accessed 28 July 2007).

World Health Organization (WHO) (2006) *WHO HIV and Infant Feeding Technical Consultation Held on Behalf of the Inter-Agency Task Team (IATT) on Prevention of HIV Infections in Pregnant Women, Mothers and their Infants*. Geneva: WHO.

Wright, C. (2001) 'Community nursing: crossing boundaries to promote health', in A. Scriven and J. Orme (eds), *Health Promotion: Professional Perspectives*, 2nd edn. Houndmills: Palgrave.

Wright, C., Parkinson, K. and Drewett, R. (2004) 'Why are babies weaned early? Data from a prospective population based cohort study', *Archives of Disease in Childhood*, 89: 813–16.

Wright, C., Parkinson, K. and Scott, J. (2006) 'Breast–feeding in a UK urban context: who breast feeds, for how long and does it matter?', *Public Health Nutrition*, 9: 686–91.

Wright, L.T., Nancarrow, C. and Kwok, P.M.H. (2001) 'Food taste preferences and cultural influences on consumption', *British Food Journal*, 103(5): 348–57.

Young, I. (2002) 'Is healthy eating all about nutrition?', *Nutrition Bulletin*, 27(1): 7–12.

Index

Added to a page number 'f' denotes a figure and 't' denotes a table.

absolute poverty 61, 151
Acheson Report 68, 69
additional needs, children with 127
adipose tissue 22, 151
adolescents
  obesity, shame and social isolation 83
  pregnancy and diet 44–5
adults, healthy eating guidelines 36–41
Adventures in Foodland 126
advertisements
  children's views about eating 112
  government reluctance to legislate
    against 11
alcohol 20, 43
amino acids 21
animal sources of protein 21
anorexia nervosa 88, 89, 90
anti-cariogenic 151
anti-cariogenic property, cheese 124
appearance, healthy diet related to 127
artefact explanations, health inequalities 68
artificial food colours 31
artificial milk 51
atopic conditions 44, 151
attachment, and eating behaviour 83,
  84, 85, 86, 90
attention deficit hyperactivity disorder
  (ADHD) 28, 81, 151
attitudes
  to female breast 49–50
  see also negative attitudes; positive
    attitudes
attunement, early feeding 84
Ayurvedic 103, 151

behaviour change approach, health
  promotion 118
behavioural explanations, health
  inequalities 68–9
behaviour(s)
  expectations at mealtimes 92
  and food additives 30, 31
  micronutrients and 27–8
  predictive of eating disorders 89
Best Value 10
binge eating 88
Black culture, and soul food 101–2

Black and minority ethnic (BME) groups,
  eating experiences 103
Black Report (1982) 9, 67, 68
blood glucose 79–80
Board of Education Circular (No. 1571) 5
body mass index (BMI) 31, 32, 151
body shape, ideas about 90
bottle-feeding 50–1
boys, obesity 31, 83
breakfast 27
breast milk 48
breastfeeding
  attachment relationships 85
  benefits 48
  calcium requirement 43
  decision to stop 50
  ethnicity and socio-economic group 49
  government initiatives to encourage 50
  HIV positive mothers 48–9
  negative attitudes to 50
  percentage figures 46
  related to indices of disadvantage 70
British Medical Association (BMA) 70
Buddhism 100t
bulimia nervosa 88, 89
Burger Boy and Sporty Girl 126–7
butter 37

caffeine 45
calcium 23, 43, 45, 124
calorie consumption 32
cancers 40
carbohydrate 20
cardiovascular disease 33, 50, 151
care, elevation of education over 145–6
caregiver-infant relationships 83–4, 86, 91
Caroline Walker Trust 13
cheese 45, 124
child poverty, reducing 71
Child Tax Credit 69
childcare
  national standards 11–12
  ten year strategy 13
childhood obesity
  calculating 31–2
  causes 32–3
  costs 33

childhood obesity *cont.*
  deficit in impulse control 80–1
  effects 33
  family approaches to food 107
  incidence 31
  link between ADHD and 81
  public service agreement to halt 136
children
  five key health outcomes 12–13
  food and eating *see* food, and eating
  hospital treatment, eating disorders 89
  micronutrients and behaviour 27–8
  nutrition and health inequalities 70–3
Children Act (2004) 13, 18
choice 9, 14, 72–3
cholecystokininin (CCK) 79
Choosing Health (DoH, 2004) 12, 16f, 137–8
Christianity 100t
Coeliac disease 30
collectivist provision, school meals 5–7, 118
comfort foods 82
Committee on Medical Aspects of Food and
    Nutrition Policy (COMA) 12, 37, 38
community dentists 138
community dieticians 138
complex carbohydrates 20, 40
compulsive competitive tendering (CCT) 8
conception, healthy eating
    guidelines 42–4
congenital abnormalities 44, 85
Consultative Group on Early childhood Care
    and Development 85
consumption, and identity 96–7
cookery skills 124
core teams, multidisciplinary 140
coronary heart disease 33, 39, 40
cortisol 82
Council for Disabled Children 127
cow's milk formulas 51
cross-cutting review
  defined 151
  of health inequalities (2002) 69
cultural beliefs, meal-time
    behaviours 122
cultural differences, in the way
    we eat 110–11
cultural explanations, health
    inequalities 68–9
cultural identity 101–2
cutlery, using 92

Davis experiment 78–9
dental caries 26, 151
dental health promotion teams 138–9
Department of Health 9, 12, 38
depression, eating and 81–3
diabetes 33, 39, 151

diet
  national targets for improving 9
  and obesity 32
dietary fibre 23, 55
dietary guidelines (FSA) 24
dietary reference values 38, 151
dieting, distinguishing eating disorders
    from 89
disabled children 127
domestic violence 74
Douglas, M. 96
drinks 123–4
dyads, mother-infant 85, 86

E additives 31
early feeding experiences, eating behaviour
    83–7
early years curriculum, promoting healthy
    eating 120–7
Early Years Foundation Stage (2008) 14, 16f
early years settings, promoting positive
    attitudes to food 90–2
eating behaviour
  eating disorders 87–90
  impulsivity 80–1
  influence of early feeding experiences 83–7
  physiological mechanisms controlling 79–80
  stress, depression and 81–3
  see also food and eating
eating disorders 87–90
Eatwell Plate 24, 38, 39–41
eco-schools 15
ecological approach, school food
    reforms 14–15
Education Act (1980) 7, 8, 9, 15, 16f
Education (Butler) Act (1944) 5–6
Education (Provision of Meals) Act (1906)
    2, 3, 15
educational approach, health promotion 118
eggs 45
empirical, defined 151
empirical approach, food and nutrition 18
empowerment approach, health promotion
    117, 118–19
energy 20, 40, 82
energy-rich foods 55, 80, 82
England
  breastfeeding rate 49
  health profile 69
EpiPens 29, 151
equality, promoting healthy eating 126–7
essential amino acids 21
essential fatty acids 22, 28
ethical consumerism 104–5
ethnicity
  and breastfeeding 49
  food, identity and 101–4

Europe, health inequalities 69–70
Every Child Matters 12–13, 18, 136
exercise, and obesity 32–3
expert authority model, health
     education 116–17
extended teams, multidisciplinary 140–1
extrinsic sugars 20

failure to thrive 86–7
families, nutritional inequalities
     within 73–4
Family Credit 7–8
family meals 54
fat-soluble vitamins 22, 27
fats 21–2, 40
'Feed me Better' campaign 10
feeding difficulties 85–6
Fitchen study (1997) 74
five-a-day school fruit and vegetables
     scheme 13
fluoride 23
foetal growth, maternal obesity 42
foetal infections, food and 45
folic acid 43, 45
food
  additives 30–1
  advertising, restrictions 11
  allergies 28, 29–30, 44
  anxiety 74
  codes 109
  and eating
    importance of multidisciplinary working
       136–40
    inculcation of children into wider world
       109–12
    policy development 1–17
    promoting positive attitudes to food
       14, 90–2, 122–3, 124–6
    researching 148–9
    symbolic significance 95–8
    see also eating behaviour; healthy eating
  and identity
    consumption 96–7
    ethnicity 101–4
    gender 106–9
    'green' or ethical consumerism 104–5
    religion 98–101
    Social class 105–6
  intolerance 28–9, 30
  packaging 97
  rationing 5, 26, 37
  sensitivity 28–30
  sustainable development strategy
     14–15, 138
food group 151
food group approach 19, 24
food poverty 72, 151

Food in Schools Programme 13
Food Standards Agency (FSA) 24, 28,
     31, 38
food-related ill health
  conditions 26–7
  costs 25
  pregnancy 45
foreign food 104, 106
Foucaultian system, self-surveillance 108

gender
  childhood obesity 31
  food, identity and 106–9
  promoting healthy eating 126–7
  see also boys; girls; men; women
genetics, and obesity 32
ghee 103
girls, obesity 31, 33
global poverty, health inequalities 61–4
global strategy (WHO), infant nutrition 47
globalization
  defined 152
  and health inequalities 64–6
glossary 151–3
glucose 20, 44, 79–80, 82
gluten intolerance 30
goat's milk formulas 51
grants, for school meals 4, 5
'green' consumerism 104–5
gross domestic product (GDP) 62, 152

health
  collective, social responsibility for 117
  initiatives, multidisciplinary working 144
health education 116–17
health inequalities 61–75
  children's nutrition 70–3
  Europe and the UK 67–70
  global poverty 61–4
  nutrition transition and globalization 64–6
  nutritional inequalities within families 73–4
Health Inequalities Unit 69
The Health of the Nation (DoH) 9, 16f
Health Profile of England (2006) 69
health promotion 116–20
  multidisciplinary working 135–50
  policy development 13–14
  programmes, developing 131–3
  WHO conference 9
health risks, obesity 33
healthy choices, supporting individuals in
     making 72–3
healthy eating
  developing health promotion programmes
     131–3
  involving parents in promoting 129–31
  listening to children 127–8

healthy eating *cont.*
    projects 13
    promoting in the early years 116, 120–7
    role of early years practitioners 139–40
    structural inequalities 118
healthy eating guidelines 36–60
    adults 36–41
    children
        1–5 years of age 54–7
        5–8 years of age 57–9
    conception and pregnancy 41–6
    infants, 0–1 years of age 46–54
healthy foods, improving access to 72
'healthy schools' 13
Healthy Start 12, 14, 16f
Hinduism 99t
HIV/AIDS 48–9, 63
homeostasis 77–9, 85
Hungry for Success (2002) 10, 11
hyperactivity 31
hypothalamus, role of 80

identity
    promoting a sense of 92
    see also food, and identity; professional
        identity
ill health *see* food-related ill health
impulsivity, and eating behaviour 80–1
inclusion, promoting healthy eating 126–7
indices of poverty and disadvantage 70, 152
individuation 85
Infant Feeding Survey (2005) 50, 70
infant mortality 46, 69
infants
    (0–1 year), healthy eating
        guidelines 46–54
    early feeding experiences and eating
        behaviour 83–7
    maternal obesity and premature 42
infections, food and foetal 45
infertility, obesity and 42
insecure attachment 90
interdisciplinary working 141
interprofessional working 145
intersectoral working 141
intrinsic sugars 20
invisibility of care work 146
iodine 27
iron 23, 27, 42–3, 45
iron deficiency anaemia 26–7
Islam 99t

joint planning 141
Judaism 99t

'kets' 112
key-person relationships 91

knowledge development, healthy
    eating 124–6
Kolkata, nutrition transition (case study) 65–6

lactose 20
lateral nucleus (LH) 80
learning, micronutrients and 27–8
life expectancy
    England and Wales 67, 69
    poorest 50 countries 62
life politics 105
Local Government Act (1986) 8
low body weight
    and conception 42
    risks to foetus 44
lymph 24, 152

McMillan, Margaret 2
macronutrients 20, 32, 152
magnesium 23
majority world 25, 152
maladaptive relationships 86
male obesity, negative effect on
    conception 42
malnutrition 2, 25, 54, 61, 63, 152
margarine 37
market principles 7–10
maternal obesity
    infertility and miscarriage 42
    poor foetal growth 42
    pregnancy complications 44
mealtimes
    behaviour expectations 92
    group identity through collective
        participation 111
    promoting healthy eating 121–3
    rules 109
meat (undercooked) 45
medical approach, health promotion 118
medical factors, obesity 32
Mediterranean-type diet 39
men
    entitlement to food within families 74
    see also male obesity
menu-planning, incorporating children's
    perspectives 128
metabolic syndrome 33
micronutrients 20, 27–8, 152
middle classes, preference for foreign
    food 106
migration, food and eating
    practices 103–4
milk
    allergy 29
    formulas (infant) 51
    guidelines for children (1–5) 55
    importance of 124

milk *cont.*
  for mothers and children under 4 years
    of age 6–7
  see also breast milk; school milk
milk sugar 20
Millennium Cohort Study 31
Millennium Goals (UN) 62
minerals 22–3, 28
miscarriage 42
monounsaturated fatty acids 21
morbidity
  defined 152
  food-related ill health 25
mortality
  defined 152
  food-related ill health 25
  rate 152
  and social class 67
  see also infant mortality; perinatal mortality
mother-infant dyads 85, 86
multiagency organizations 141
multidisciplinary working 135–50
  benefits and barriers 143–7
  case study 142–3
  explained 140–3
importance in children's food and eating
    136–40
importance of research 147–8

National Children's Bureau (NCB) 70
National Curriculum 14
National Healthy School Standard 13
natural and social selection, health
    inequalities 68
negative attitudes, to breastfeeding 50
network associations 141
neural tube 152
neural tube defects 43, 44
non-organic failure to thrive (NOFT) 86–7
non-starch polysaccarides 23
nursery case study, meals provision 56–7
nursery guidelines, healthy eating 54–7
nutrients 19, 20–4, 152
nutrition
  and health inequalities 70–3
  national targets for improving 9
  role in development of adults and children
    25–8
  science of 26
nutrition transition 64–5, 152
  case study 65–6
nutritional inequalities
  reducing 71–3
  within families 73–4
nutritional requirements, COMA
    estimation 37
nutritional standards, school meals 5, 12, 15

obesity
  defined 152
  depression 83
  preference for energy-rich foods 80
  rates 31
  see also childhood obesity; male obesity;
    maternal obesity
obesogenic, defined 153
obesogenic diet 65
obsession 88
oily fish 43
Oliver, Jamie 10
oral disease 26
Ottawa Charter (WHO, 1986) 9, 117

parents, involving in promoting healthy
    eating 129–31
partnerships
  multidisciplinary 141
  with parents 129–31
pâté 45
peanuts 44, 45
pedagogic meal 122–3
perinatal mortality 42, 153
Personal, Social and Health Education
    (PSHE) 14
pf glucose 82
philanthropic concern (pre-1906) 2–3
physiological drives 77
physiological mechanisms
  consumption of energy-rich foods 82
  control of food intake 79–80
play, role in developing positive
    attitudes 125–6
policy development 1–17
  philanthropic concern (pre-1906) 2–3
  residual service (1906–Second World War)
    3–5
  universal service (1944–79) 5–7
  return to the market (1980–96) 7–10
  safeguarding futures (1997
    onwards) 10–15
  timeline 16f
polyunsaturated fatty acids 21
popular culture, sweets and 112
positive attitudes, to food, encouraging
    and promoting 14, 90–2, 122–3, 124–6
post-structuralist, defined 153
post-structuralist approaches, to food and
    eating 96–8
poverty
  child nutrition 70
  health inequalities 68
  see also absolute poverty; child poverty;
    food poverty; global poverty; indices
    of poverty and disadvantage; relative
    poverty

power
  issue of, in food and eating 109
  multidisciplinary working 145
pre-conception, healthy eating during 42–4
pre-eclampsia 44, 153
pregnancy
  healthy eating during 44–6
  public education programme 12
premature babies, maternal low body
    weight 42
preventative approach, health promotion 118
professional adulthood 144–5
professional identity 145
professionalism, elevation of education over
    caring 145–6
'progress' milks 51
protein 20–1, 27
psychological difficulties, obesity and 33
psychological mechanisms, eating
    behaviour 80–90
public education programme, pregnant
    mothers and carers 12
public health, national targets for improving 9
Public Sector Food Procurement Initiative 138
public service agreements (PSAs) 69, 136, 153
Punjabi women, food classification 103
pyramid guideline, healthy eating 38–9

radical health promotion 119
Rastafarianism 100t
reinforcers 82
relationships
  development, during mealtimes 121
  see also caregiver-infant relationship
relative poverty 61, 153
religion, food, identity and 98–101
representation, of caregivers 83
research, multidisciplinary working 147–8
residual school meals service 3–5, 118
responsibility, early feeding process 85
rhythm, in food and eating 96
rickets 27
risk factors, eating disorders 90
Royal College of Psychiatrists (RCoP)
    88, 89
Royal Commission on Physical
    Deterioration 2

salt 40, 58
saturated fatty acids 21, 32
Saving Lives: Our Healthier Nation (DoH)
    13, 16f
School Food Trust 12, 16f
school guidelines, healthy eating 57–9
school meals
  competitive tendering for catering
    contracts 8

school meals cont.
  'Feed me Better' campaign 10
  grants for 4, 5
  policy
    absence of child's voice in relation to 15
    factors impacting on (1944–79) 5
  provision
    collectivist 5–7, 118
    factors leading to introduction of 2–3
    reining in of state 7–8
    residual 3–5, 118
  standards
    new (2006) 58
    nutritional 5, 12, 15
    reinstatement of minimum 11
School Meals Campaign (1992) 10
school milk
  LEA obligation to provide 5–6
  withdrawal of free 7
School Milk Scheme 4
school nurses 139
school performance, and nutrition 27, 28
schools
  health promotion in 119–20
  see also 'healthy schools'
Scientific Advisory Committee on Nutrition
    (SACN) 38
Scotland
  breastfeeding rate 49
  school meals provision 2
secure attachment 83
self-esteem, promoting 92
self-identity see identity
semi-skimmed milk 55
senior dental officers 138–9
service agreements 141
shellfish (raw) 45
Sikhism 99t
skills development, healthy
    eating 124–6
skimmed milk 55
snacks 123–4
social anthropology 95, 153
social change approach, health
    promotion 119
social class
  food, identity and 105–6
  mortality 67
Social Security Act (1986) 7
socio-economic group, and
    breastfeeding 49
sodium benzoate 30, 31
sodium glutamate 30
sodium metabisulphite 30–1
Somalian diet, and cultural identity 102
soul-food 101–2
soya milk formulas 51

special educational needs, children with 127
speciesism 105
stomach size, control of food intake 79
stress, eating and 81–3
structural inequalities, in relation to healthy eating 118
structuralist, defined 153
structuralist approaches, to food and eating 95–6
subjectivity 96
sugars 20, 40
Sure Start 12, 69
sustainable development strategy 14–15, 138
sweet-eating 108, 111–12
symbolic significance, food and eating 95–8

Tackling Health Inequalities, a Programme for Action (2003) 69
tartrazine 30
teams, multidisciplinary 141
teenagers *see* adolescents
Ten Year Strategy for Childcare 13
Thatcher, Margaret 7
trace elements 23
trans fatty acids 22
tuning-in, to children's perspectives 128
Turning the Tables (2005) 14
type 2 diabetes 33

UNICEF 47
United Kingdom
government guidelines, healthy eating 39–41
health inequalities 67–9
see also England; Scotland

United Nations
Children's Fund 25, 48
Convention on the Rights of the Child 9
Millennium Declaration 62
United States, healthy eating guidelines 38–9
universal school meal service 5–7

vegetarianism 21, 105
vitamin A 43, 45
vitamin D 27, 45
vitamin D deficiency 27, 45
vitamins 22, 28
vouchers, (Healthy Start) 12, 14

water 23–4, 124
water soluble vitamins 22
weaning 51–4
weight *see* low body weight; obesity
Welfare Food Scheme (1940) 6–7, 12
welfare state provision, Conservative attack on 8
women
experience of food and eating within families 73–4
risk of eating disorders 88–9
and vegetarianism 105
see also maternal obesity; mother-infant dyads
Working for Children (DWP, 2007) 71
World Health Organization (WHO) 9, 47, 62